POSITIVE
IMPACT
GOLF

Incorporating The World Renowned
'Danse du Golf' Movement

HEALTH WARNING

**Applying What You
Read in this Book Will
Seriously Enhance the
Enjoyment of Your Golf!**

Brian Sparks

Positive Impact Golf
Manston Golf Centre
Manston Rd.
Manston
Kent CT12 5BE

First published by AuthorHouse 6/18/2010

ISBN: 978-0-9928534-0-2

"These days it seems like a lot of people write books based on theory. They sound good, they promise a lot but in the end they tend to disappoint. They fail what I call the 'real world' test. Are they written by people of genuine real world experience who have been at the coal face day in day out actually working with their ideas? Most have not.

The book that you are about to read passes that test with flying colours. This is a book written for YOU the golfer by a coach who has clearly spent his life passionately involved in coaching and the processes involved in helping you to play better golf. And perhaps more importantly to get more enjoyment from the game. Read this book with an open mind. Allow yourself to leave some of your past conditioning behind and enjoy the opportunity to view the game from a totally different and exciting perspective. Put your golf in the safe hands of Brian Sparks and I feel certain that you will move your game to a level that you perhaps didn't consider possible."
—Karl Morris, European Tour Mind Coach to Darren Clark and Lee
   Westwood

"Brian Sparks has done a very nice job in helping golfers with the most important aspect of the game – the mental side."
—Tim Gallwey, Author of the Inner Game books on Tennis, Golf, Skiing,
   Music, Work, Winning & Stress

"Until I read Positive Impact Golf I was a good athlete in most sports but I was so frustrated by my inability to play good golf that I only played when I had to. That all changed in a matter of a few weeks by applying the book's simple message of a more natural swinging motion. It demystified a lot of the technical stuff I had learnt and I now love my swing and the way I hit the ball. I have also reduced my score by 12 shots a round!"
— John P Strelecky - International Best-Selling Author- 'The Big Five for
   Life' – 'Leadership's Greatest Secret,' 'The Why Cafe,' 'Life Safari.'

"Positive Impact Golf has given me a golf swing I didn't think existed. I'm straighter, more consistent, have gained 15 yards in length and am now down to 7 handicap. Amazingly, all this with less effort, less thought and more relaxation. Heaven!"
— Joe Sach – 33 year-old BA Pilot

"More and more sports coaches are realising that the mental and emotional state of a performer is in many cases more significant than their technique for their success. This calls for a new approach to coaching. Brian's new book illustrates and emphasizes this well and should be read by teachers and players alike."
— Sir John Whitmore, PhD – CEO Performance Consultants International
   & Author of Coaching For Performance

"Rarely does a book on coaching remember that all those reading may not be the same! Brian successfully communicates his knowledge from a lifetime of playing and coaching the game and from studying at first hand the best coaches in the world, whilst ensuring that you are fully involved in your own development. It stands alone as a great story of the experiences of a tournament professional and coach and for those seeking personal progression in their careers and performance. Positive Impact Golf will not only help you achieve your potential but will transform your experience of the learning process."
— Karl Steptoe, Psychologist & PGA Professional

"I was once invited to spend a day with David Leadbetter and a group of a dozen Pro's. David got us to change our swings dramatically; it was as though he could see into our mechanics and force us to change our bad habits. The difference with Brian is that he can "see" what is going on in both our body and our mind. It is this ability to find what causes us to make un-

natural or ineffective movements that is at the core of how he helps golfers find their own natural and correct swing. This discovery provides them with the awareness to develop the solution in a natural, reliable and permanent way. Positive Impact Golf combines technique and psychology in the easiest and most effective way I have ever witnessed."
— Philip Sparks, PGA Professional & Qualified Golf Course Architect

"Since reading a small part of Positive Impact Golf published as a report on the 6 Key Basics I am hitting the ball further and straighter. Everything else I had read before seemed to suit young athletes and not me. I am 78 years old, have 2 new knees and have recently reduced my handicap from 20 to 18. I can't wait to read the whole book!"
— Bill Haffenden- Retired (Bromley UK)

"Positive Impact Golf is more about finding the real 'source' of any problem, and not making a judgement from any visual impression when a golf swing deviates from a so called 'textbook' swing. This is about quickly breaking down the pupil's misconceptions about the golf swing and then, once free of some of these 'tension building' theories, helping them to create a relaxed and more natural swing.

22 years ago, I was a successful tour player. I then had a very dramatic loss of form, and have struggled hopelessly ever since. I have had many lessons, but each time, I not only didn't improve, but got considerably worse. About 3 weeks after my first lesson with Brian, I am not only back at my best, I also understand why, and my swing is 100% natural, and amazingly, I have done it all without any conscious effort, or even a swing thought."
— PGA Pro Richard Fish, finished 2nd on the 1988 Safari Circuit to Vijay
    Singh

Table of Contents

Acknowledgements

My thanks to:

Bee, for your love, support, encouragement, patience and understanding during my selfish writing period.

Michel Perroux, as the major influence in my life to understanding the limitations of traditional teaching methods and showing me the tremendous value of positive thinking.

John Ayress, for inciting me to go public and for your invaluable help with proof reading.

My sisters Pat and Brenda, and my brother Philip, for your belief in me.

Peter Allen, for your input, friendship, encouragement and unique way of looking at the world.

Roger Mace, for giving me the opportunity to make a career in golf and opening my mind to a professional attitude at such a young age.

John Norsworthy, the first golf coach who inspired me to see golf in a less technical way.

Timothy Gallwey, such a major influence on the way I coach.

Kjell Enhager, Ernest Jones, Bobby Jones, Fred Shoemaker, Dr Joseph Parent, Dr Bob Rotella, Sir John Whitmore, Michael Murphy, and Stan Utley for the content of all their books.

John P. Strelecky, for your invaluable advice and for helping me to get this to print. Your advice to ask Jana Rade, Creative Director at Impact Studios, to design the book's cover and interior pages was a master stroke! A big 'thank you' to Jana for her brilliance and patience.

All the guys I've worked with over the years whose input has been invaluable.

Most importantly, all the people who have sought my help to learn or improve their golf over the last 40 years. I have learnt so much from you all and you are the true inspiration for this book.

Finally, thank you for purchasing my book. I have written it with the intention of providing some positive input into the way you look at your own golfing potential and helping you to get even more enjoyment from this beautiful game.

Authors Notes

I am a right-handed golfer and I have chosen to use the right-handed terms throughout most of the book. I found it ungainly to do otherwise and I apologise to the left-handed reader who is obliged to translate every right to left and vice-versa. I have, however, used the expressions 'front' foot or 'leading' arm instead of 'left' wherever it seemed appropriate.

I have also chosen to use 'he' in many cases as again, the use of 'he and/or she' is rather cumbersome. I apologise to the female reader but would assure her that the content of this book will be at least as beneficial to her as it will be to the male golfer.

I made myself a promise many years ago that I would always use everyday words and terms and not fall into the trap of using complex terminology and jargon in my coaching sessions. I will do my utmost to be faithful to that promise in this book.

Each chapter starts with a personal quote from me.

There is no sound so sweet,
No sight so spine tingling,
No feeling so good,
As a well struck golf shot.

THIS book is dedicated to the millions of golfers who have been misled into believing basic concepts of golf swing technique which actually prevent them from swinging a golf club and playing the game in a way that is true to their personal flexibility, age, and individual body rhythms. The concepts in this book have the power to make the game much easier, much more enjoyable and to help you plug into the natural abilities that all human beings possess.

BEFORE
YOU START
READING

Let's Get Interactive

I HAVE written this book with the sole purpose of helping golfers to view the art of swinging a golf club and hitting a golf ball in a different light. You will read in these pages that I am convinced that certain traditional concepts make it difficult for you to tap into your natural ability to swing the club in a relaxed, rhythmical and effective manner with any degree of consistency.

You will see that you can achieve astounding progress simply by letting go of these misconceptions and embracing a more natural way of playing the game.

In order for you to draw maximum benefit from reading it, and before I go any further, I strongly suggest you start a notebook to record anything you find meaningful in the following pages. Start by writing down your thoughts on how you should swing a golf club.

Yes, do it NOW! If you haven't got a notebook go and get a sheet of paper and a pen or pencil and write it all down. Go on, do it now or the opportunity to register your beliefs before being in any way influenced by this book will be lost! The comparison between your thoughts now and the way they may evolve throughout the book will provide greater insight and options for the way you choose to play the game in the future.

If you are just starting to play, you may not have much to put down but that's fine. For you, this book will help to avoid putting complicated and outdated barriers in the way of developing a simple and natural way of playing and you will, I trust, understand the philosophy as the pages unfold.

On the other hand, if you have played golf for any length of time I would like you to write down the main points you would focus on when giving some advice to a beginner, someone who has never held a club in their hands before. This person has no idea how to swing a club so your advice is likely to be very influential and long remembered. All novices are particularly sensitive to the things they learn at the very first stage in any new subject or domain.

As you read further into the book, and learn more about 'La Danse du Golf,' the comparison between your thoughts and mine will be of great value. If you take the time to do it right now (yes, straight away), you will benefit to a maximum degree. Take your time. Don't rush. If you can't think of anything to start off with just be patient and let your mind sift through all the information you have gained over the years and let the words come. If they are in your subconscious it is normal that they will take some time to pop in to your conscious mind. A cornerstone of my philosophy is that the thoughts and beliefs that reside in your subconscious are the ones in the driving seat of your way of playing golf, not the ones you may be actively thinking about and aware of before and during each shot.

Once you've finished, and it doesn't matter if you've written a few words or many, I would like you to answer the following more specific questions. You may well have covered these already. That's OK.

These questions are all prefixed by 'what would you tell a beginner about...'

- their head – (a) generally in the swing, (b)in the backswing, (c) after impact
- their eyes
- their arms – (a) in the backswing, (b) through and after impact
- their front foot in the backswing (left foot for a right handed player)
- the line the club head should take in the first foot of the backswing
- the line the club head takes as it moves back through the ball and for the first foot after impact
- when they should cock their wrists in the backswing
- what point in the swing should the club head reach its greatest speed
- what they should do after a bad shot
- what they should do after a round of golf

Now give yourself a score from 0 to 10 for how good you are at the following aspects of your swing, zero being poor and ten being excellent:
- how good am I at swinging with no effort
- how good am I at playing with a relaxed swing
- how good is my rhythm
- how good is my balance at the end of my swing
- how well do I get through to a full finish

Please do this before you read on or the opportunity to compare what you will learn with what you have done before will be lost. The understanding and knowledge contained in this book will give you new and fresh options for your future enjoyment.

Now, keep this in a safe place as it will be important later and keep writing notes as you read. How many times have I read a book and then had to read it again because I didn't make notes the first time?

Introduction

"40 years of experience helping thousands of golfers of all standards to learn and improve their game has taught me an easier and more natural way of playing this wonderful game. It is time to go public!"

T HE average person is more than capable of playing the game in an easier and more natural manner. In this book I will demonstrate and help you discover a new perspective on your true potential. I am convinced that the average handicap has not improved either in Britain or the USA over the last four decades because modern teaching over-complicates what is, in essence, a very simple affair. Add to this the indoctrination of all new golfers to conform to outdated and complex principles and you will easily understand why I am determined to lead golf coaching in a new, simple and inherently more natural direction.

In these pages you will see why you play well sometimes without knowing how and you will be able to control your game instead of being controlled by it. You will gain the tools to play consistently better golf because you will know how to find your natural swing and how to shed the false and over-technical version you have been indoctrinated to use. You will de-clutter your golfing mind and become more confident and positive about your game.

I founded 'Positive Impact Golf' to help release the average golfer from the interference of limiting beliefs from which he or she is unwittingly suffering. Since discovering the power of our belief system, I am yet to find a golfer at any level of the game who is completely free of negative and self-limiting beliefs that affect how they swing the club and how they play the game.

Your potential to perform any task in life can be blocked by interference which comes in many forms. I will be talking to you about this subject in the following pages both with regard to the fundamentals of the golf swing and to the power of a positive mindset in your game. Swinging the club to your potential and consistently hitting well struck shots is a matter of getting out of your own way both physically and mentally.

When you start to apply the Six Core Swing Basics contained in these pages and to develop a new attitude to your bad shots you will have the tools to benefit fully from your latent ability. You will be able to reduce your handicap by at least 20%, recognise tension in your swing and reduce it by 50% or more, reduce the physical effort you employ, increase your 'feel' for the game, prolong your golfing life and, most important of all, enjoy your game more than ever before.

Your golf will lose much of its frustration and anxiety when you learn about the importance of a positive attitude to bad shots and how to get into the right state to play your best golf more often.

Swinging a golf club and hitting a ball are not difficult. They do become so however, when people apply themselves in ways that undermine their latent talent and inhibit their ability to use it effectively.

As Fred Shoemaker wrote in his excellent book, Extraordinary Golf, *"Consider the possibility that you may be far more able than you think and that when you let go of self-interference and increase your aware-ness, you will see exceptional ability emerge."*

We play our best golf when we are swinging the club well whether it is with a driver, an iron or even a putter. When that happens the game feels so easy. But this sentiment quickly reverses and leaves us baffled and frustrated when we play badly. Why does hitting a golf ball go from being such a simple affair one minute to being so complicated and dif-ficult the next? Sometimes this happens from one day to another, from front nine to back nine, from one hole to another or even from one shot to the next.

It is a simple fact that we don't think too much when we are playing well. In fact, the less we think the better we play! However, as soon as we hit a bad shot we are tempted to ask 'why?' and so start to create our own downfall by consciously trying to correct the things we imagine we are doing wrong. But can we really put our finger on the right fault? Let me explain.

Imagine that you have just topped a shot, in other words the ball hasn't got off the ground. Everyone tells you that you've lifted your head. So, what are you going to do other than try and keep your head down longer on the next shots? But, does it work? If it does, surely you will know forever how to stop it happening again? Can you put your hand up and say that you don't top shots anymore? In the many years I have spent studying golfers I have rarely seen anyone hit the top of the ball due to lifting their head, despite what everyone tells them! By applying themselves to this erroneous analysis they end up staying down too long and blocking any chance they have of swinging smoothly through to a poised and correct finish. What's more, it doesn't cure the topped shot. The plain truth is that golfers tend to misdirect their efforts in correcting problems that don't exist.

We play better golf when we are relaxed and move well. We play badly when we feel stiff and static. Is it possible to stay still and move dynamically at one and the same time? I doubt it. Golf coaching should focus on this essential aspect of the game and thus help golfers to develop more confidence in movement. Muscle tension is the major interference in golf.

Whilst seeking to conform to recognised and traditional swing fundamentals, you may actually be increasing difficulty by unwittingly adding tension to your swing. Inconsistency ensues and your ability to express your full talent becomes blocked. You are literally getting in your own way.

We all have the ability to swing the club with good rhythm. When you hit a purple patch doesn't it feel easy? Aren't you struck by how little effort it requires to hit lovely shots that ping off the club head and soar into the air, seemingly hanging in space for much longer than usual?

Golf teachers and coaches around the world recognise the need to help you correct your swing faults and to improve your swing. But the traditional corrective is a positional one. The thinking is, if your swing looks better from a technical viewpoint then you must hit better shots and play better golf. This philosophy is flawed because it doesn't respect your body's natural rhythms or the flow of motion that even the word 'swing' intimates. I believe totally in the quote from Ron Frankel, an advocate of the Ernest Jones' school of teaching, when he states, *"Motion is essential in the golf swing but you can't dissect motion into parts and still have motion. Therefore, you can't dissect the golf swing into parts and still have a swing."*

Ernest Jones was one of the most famous English Golf Pro's to have ever taught golf in the USA. He published his book 'Swing the Club Head' in 1937 and I am convinced that golf teaching has failed to build on his beliefs but has rather become immersed in an abyss of technical, complex and unnatural principles. Unfortunately, I have seen no progress in how the average player sees the basic fundamentals of the golf swing in the last forty years. At the same time, the quality of the clubs we use and the balls we hit has improved out of all recognition.

In general, good players and professionals have improved their swings and part of the reason is that they aren't controlled by the same requirement to conform as the average golfer. Their scores, by comparison, have improved quite dramatically. Why? Read on and you will find out.

Have you ever been told that you are too stiff when you play? Have you ever been told that you don't turn your shoulders enough on the back swing? Have you ever wondered why you can't keep your balance like you see when good players swing the club? Do you know why you can't get through to a full and proper finish like all good players do? Have you ever asked yourself why the golf swing is so complicated? I will answer these questions.

I hope that you will be persuaded that you have been worshipping false gods and I sincerely hope that you will not only change your ideas but that you will help me to change one of the greatest ills in golf: the amount of unsolicited, confusing and debilitating advice that you receive from well-meaning friends whenever you have a golf club in your hands. You can also help me to achieve Bobby Jones' dream of a more simple approach to the golf swing as you will read in his quote at the end of this introduction; words that he wrote in his 1960 book 'Golf is My Game.'

Having given you my take on the real basics of the golf swing I will go on to tell you my personal story so that you may better understand from where I am coming and how I discovered a new world. This book is not an autobiography but I believe that some background information about me and how some early mistakes, followed by a process of changing my attitude to technique, had such an important impact on my coaching philosophy. You will see that my coaching beliefs are based on personal experience, not only in forty years of coaching thousands of golfers, but also in the evolution of my own game. The basic exercise, 'La Danse du Golf,' comes from my time as a coach in France. The spelling of the word 'dance' may have already intrigued you. The word for 'dance' is the same in French but is spelt with an 's' not a 'c.' My French clientele came up with the name for this exercise that encapsulates what I see as the 6 basic principles of a good golf swing. It is only right and proper that their influence on my fundamental philosophy be reflected in the name given to a simple movement that will show you that you naturally possess all the required components of a good golf swing. Moreover, it will help you FEEL the difference between two completely different and opposing ways of developing your swing. It will give you choices and options that you may have never considered or been aware of before. It is only when information is translated into FEEL that coaching becomes totally successful and sustainable.

The 19th century American essayist and poet, Ralph Waldo Emerson, said *"Do not go where the path may lead, go instead where there is no path and leave a trail."* At the start of my career I did, indeed, follow the path. I knew no better. I then deviated from it and discovered a whole new world. It was as if I had gone through a door into a foreign land. I have been following my instincts ever since and have found many new doors. This book is all about the trail I hope to have left behind me and the adventure of the journey. At certain times my trail has undoubtedly crossed those left by other coaches who have deviated from the classic route and I am more and more convinced that those of us who have left the traditional 'path' work much of the time in parallel. You will find a list of publications by some of these people at the end of the book and some of their quotes in these pages. You will find that many of their words were written years ago and indicate that, sophisticated as we contemporary golf teachers think we are, maybe we have just failed to listen to our predecessors and have lost our way. Even worse, maybe we have conspired to make the game more difficult for the average player.

If you've ever found the game of golf difficult or frustrating you will discover that you can't do some of the traditional things and play to your potential. You can't keep making the same mistakes and expect to suddenly find the 'secret of golf.'

My comment about 'going public' actually comes from one of my closest friends, John, who once innocently (?) asked me, "When are you going to go public?" This, then, is my attempt to bring my ideas to a wider audience.

Of course, on the one hand, those who are still firmly following the traditional path will find this book uncomfortable or even threatening. On the other hand, those of you who have already started your own trails will find some common ground. My intentions are quite simple; to help others to avoid the false roads I have taken and, most importantly, to help golfers learn more effectively and faster. As Emerson also said, *"Knowledge exists to be imparted."*

I would ask those readers who find that my thoughts are similar to theirs to get in touch. It is about time we got together to form a counter-opinion to the traditionalists and thus have a greater impact on how the game is played by the average golfer. It is also time to put a stop to the 'position' focused way of coaching, or *"the joined-up-dots method"* as the American Pro, Stan Utley, calls it in his book 'The Art of the Short Game'. Only then can we influence and improve the average handicap in the future.

Please enjoy the read.

Brian Sparks

"It seems obvious to me that writing about the golf swing has become too technical and complicated, and even the most earnest teaching professional presents the game to his pupil as a far more difficult thing than it really is. It is equally obvious that what the game needs most if it is to grow in popularity is a simplification of teaching routines which will present a less formidable aspect to the beginner, and offer to the average player a rosier prospect of improvement."

—Bobby Jones – 1930 Grand Slam
  Winner - 'Golf Is My Game' (1960)

Part 1:
Liberating Your Swing Potential

Movement and the Big Six

> Q: "How can I avoid hitting bad shots?"
> A: "Address the ball and don't move.
> Now, stay like this and you'll never hit a
> bad shot again!"

LA DANSE DU GOLF

FOR those who have already played, even if only a few times, it is essential to commence by finding out what they believe, just as I have done with you at the start of this book. By doing this before going through 'La Danse du Golf', each individual will have the opportunity of comparing what they do with what they believe and then choosing which things to retain and which parts they wish to change. Effective coaching in any domain should provide this kind of real choice and subsequent empowerment.

Look at Sheila in photos 1, 2 and 3. Try copying them now if you can. Compare her position as she moves through pictures 2 and 3. In French this is called the 'va et viens,' (the going and coming), or as we might

Photo 1   Photo 2   Photo 3

say, the coming and going. She has made a rotational shift away from her starting position before moving back through it to achieve a finish position, again with good rotational shift in the direction that she would want to hit the ball. As you copy this movement make sure that your feet turn in both directions and don't just lift up. Lifting your feet straight in front of you without turning will limit your ability to rotate. We are looking to get every joint in our body turning in order to achieve a full and comfortable rotation with good weight transference.

This most simple exercise is designed to give golfers the feeling of a golf swing. Do not underestimate it as its simplicity hides a high degree of effectiveness. It will help you to feel, know and appreciate the natural flow of rhythm that your body possesses. It is based on the belief that motion is essential and that the degree required by each person can be decided naturally. It is a movement totally devoid of traditional tension and thus provides a comfortable antidote to the classic 'coil like a spring' method that so many golfers just accept as being normal.

I am convinced that the golf swing is often presented as an awkward, technical and unnatural movement and that this alone is responsible for a huge loss of beginners who had the potential to reap full enjoyment of the game but gave up at the first few hurdles.

'La Danse du Golf' will soon allow you to translate all the individual thoughts and all the new knowledge into one whole entity; the feeling of what you are looking to achieve. All good coaching must arrive at this result.

The Big 6 Basics

Most coaches consider the golf swing to be a 'throwing' movement. OK, we throw the club at the same time as striking the ball but I totally agree with this concept. As you are making 'La Danse du Golf' movement, as in the photos, you will feel that your body is **TURNING** and that your **WEIGHT** is **SHIFTING** from foot to foot. This would be the basis of a natural movement of throwing a stone in a pond or throwing the discus in athletics or a ball in baseball or cricket. Have you ever tried throwing a ball as far as you can whilst standing still? Would you do this and keep your head still and your arm straight? If the 'coil' theory was so effective why do discus throwers not stand rooted to the spot whilst keeping their heads still and their feet static? It just isn't logical, is it?

What else can we feel in 'La Danse du Golf' movement? Well, you could say that it is like a little dance routine. After all, we are going to make the same sort of movement whatever club we have in our hands. Yes, I will agree that a driver swing is not exactly the same as a nine-iron but it differs because of the length, lie and weight of the club and the subsequent distance you stand from the ball. You will still need to turn and transfer your weight even if the amount would be more with the driver than the nine-iron. The truth is that all golf swings should belong to the same family whether a driver or an iron or a full shot, half shot or chip.

If you ask yourself what are the basics of dancing or what assets marvellous dancers like Fred Astaire might need to perform so well, what might we come up with? Undoubtedly, a good sense of **RHYTHM** will be essential, as would a good sense of **BALANCE**. A good level of **COORDINATION** wouldn't go amiss either, be that the synchronisation of the various parts of his own body or the timing of his movements with his dance partner. In golfing terms our dance partner is the golf club. I've never seen a more relaxed dancer than Fred who always look totally at ease and, please excuse me, I prefer to go back to my time in France for a more suitable word to describe the suppleness he displayed, **SOUPLESSE**. 'Souplesse' is a more expressive word that rolls more elegantly off the tongue than the English suppleness.

Any top golfer you care to mention displays these six attributes in plenty. Have you ever seen a great golfer who keeps his chest face-on to the ball in the back swing and who doesn't shift his weight from foot to foot? Have you ever seen a great golfer who doesn't have good rhythm and balance? Have you ever seen a great golfer who is uncoordinated and stiff? I leave you to answer these questions for yourself.

I once watched Seve Ballesteros for an hour on the practice ground at La Manga. I was on holiday with a group of members from Staverton Park and one of them, Gerald, a four-handicapper, was with me. Afterwards, we went back to hitting some shots ourselves. No, I don't know why, but Seve didn't repay the compliment by coming to watch us! Anyway, I found myself mimicking his rhythm and turned to tell Gerald, who was behind me, just how fantastically and easily I was hitting the ball. He was just about to hit a shot so I watched him before talking. Well, it was amazing. I had known him for a couple of years by then and had never seen him swing so well. The fact is that we had both been influenced by Seve's superb rhythm and had some-how absorbed some of it.

You see, we all possess the six basics to some degree or other. For example, we simply couldn't exist without a sense of rhythm. How would life be if we had no balance or no coordination? Whilst I know that the average golfer is not a young athlete and is probably unlikely to see the low side of fifty again, even he or she has some flexibility. I believe that the established method of swinging a club (still head, straight arm and static front foot, see below) actually compromises your ability to swing the club well. It limits your mobility whilst cre-ating unacceptably high levels of tension. Let me not mince my words in one respect.

Tension is at the root of all evil in golf. It steals your feel and robs you of your talent. The traditional 'coil' method, whereby you are en-couraged to turn your shoulders against a resisting lower body, may well be feasible for flexible and athletic low handicappers and pros but it makes basic rotation difficult for the majority of players and can increase tension to destructive levels.

If you have any form of back trouble or any pulled muscles please take great care to read through the next section before trying what I suggest. You may care to read the words, look at the photos and just imagine the consequences. You might just find out why playing golf gives you a bad back or simply aggravates your back problems.

How To Feel Unnatural And Stiff

Let me show you exactly what I mean by tension. Go back to 'La Danse du Golf' and get yourself into the position in photo 2. Take an internal snapshot of how this feels and call it A. Now start again keeping your front foot glued to the ground as Mick is doing in photo 4. Your heel, in particular, must not lift at all. Stop there for a while and feel what is happening in your body. Let's call this position B. Now compare this with how A felt. Are you comfortable and relaxed? Surely not! Now start again with your leading arm straight out in front of you as in photo 5 and then turn as in photo 6 still keeping your foot on the ground and your arm straight. Again, make the same comparison with this position, which we'll call C. Don't stay in this position too long as you may become quite uncomfortable. Now, let your arm drop and relax for a moment before the tension does you any harm.

Start again, as before with arm straight and foot down, but adding 'la piece de resistance' i.e. keeping your head absolutely still, as in photo 7. Your eyes should look out over where the ball would be and, if you were wearing spectacles they shouldn't move a millimetre. This may sound a bit extreme but, after all, this is exactly what your subconscious belief has been trying to get your body to conform to all this time. Call this position D and again compare how you're feeling with position A. Look at Mick's left shoulder in photo 7. See how much tension there is compared to picture 6. This is what happens when you try to keep things still. You create tension.

Please let go quickly as you can so easily pull a muscle in your back or do yourself some other injury. Now go back to the full version of 'La Danse du Golf' and compare the ease of making the movement with

Photo 4   Photo 5

Photo 6   Photo 7

the six basics of Turning, Weight Shift, Rhythm, Balance, Coordination and Souplesse. Depending on your personal level of physical flexibility, you will have felt how easy they are in 'La Danse du Golf' and just how they are made difficult when applying the '3 Deadly Don'ts' (still head, straight arm, static left foot) each stage of which makes these basics progressively more difficult.

Noah is thirteen years old and has only just started to play golf. Despite his youthful flexibility photo 8 shows how traditional thinking can produce awkwardness and add unnaturally high levels of tension to even a young person's swing. He is totally relaxed in photo 9.

Have a look at photos 10 & 11 of Jill who's experiencing the best golf she's ever played since learning 'La Danse du Golf.' It has helped her achieve a more natural and relaxed way of playing. She suffers a chronic bad back and had resorted to using an iron off the tee for the last 10 years. This was made all the more difficult as she plays on a long championship links course where distance off the tee is at a premium. She now uses her driver with confidence and is enjoying her golf more than for years, and she can play without hurting her back.

Since embracing the concept of free footwork and softer arms, Mick (photo 12), a 5 handicap player is finding the game easier and hitting the ball consistently much further with less effort. Most interestingly, he no longer suffers from pains in his groin and right shoulder that were direct consequences of the 'coil' method which he had learnt before.

Later, in the section titled 'Where do our natural abilities go when we play golf,' I will be asking you to imagine some golfers as they arrive at their club. You will see how they are dressed and what sort of equipment they take out of their cars and you will notice that they are reasonably well coordinated and don't fall over as they walk to the clubhouse. Most of us possess natural levels of rhythm, balance, coordination and flexibility. The overwhelming evidence is, after watching and helping golfers for forty years, that normal people don't, in general, display these abilities when they play golf. One of the most startling sessions I ever experienced was when coaching a thirty-year

Photo 8

Photo 9

Photo 12

Photo 10

Photo 11

old woman in France. She told me that she was a very good dancer and played good tennis but really struggled with the game of golf. In fact, it was so difficult that she had been playing for a couple of years and had accepted that she only had the energy for nine holes. For her, playing eighteen holes was just too exhausting.

Of course, this immediately alerted me to some anomaly. Why was an apparently fit young woman having such difficulties with golf? Well,

41

as soon as she addressed her first ball it was obvious that she had been told to apply the '3 Deadly Don'ts' and was so tight that I could see the stress and pain on her face even before she started to swing the club away from the ball! She had been such a good student to the people she had listened to that she had the straightest left arm I have ever seen and swung the club back with hardly any body movement at all. She was tired after just a couple of shots. Although she found it challenging to go through 'La Danse du Golf' routine she quickly understood the false nature of her beliefs and I could see the tension disappear before my very eyes as her stiff and awkward swing was transformed into one of the most fluid, relaxed and elegant movements that I had ever seen. Yes, this is the power of 'La Danse du Golf' to radically change the way you play golf. What was more satisfying was to hear her tell me, only a week later, that she had enjoyed a full round of eighteen holes for the first time in ages and felt as fresh as a daisy at the end.

A simple benefit of the freedom of movement for women which comes with 'La Danse du Golf' was highlighted to me for the first time in my career just recently by Sue. I promised to include in my book the fact that letting her head and feet move allowed her to swing her chest out of the way of the swing of her arms in her back swing for the first time in her golfing life!

Origins Of 'La Danse Du Golf'

My first inkling that more movement was not only a good thing but was also freely available to most of us, came about when I was playing in a practice round for a Midland PGA tournament in the early 1980's with one of my Assistant Pro's, Charlie.

I had coached Charlie since meeting him as a junior member at Barton-on-Sea in 1974 and had seen an extraordinary potential in him from the first day. Over the years he developed a great golf swing and had become a really good player and wonderful striker of the ball. Anyone who knew him will agree that he had great ability and could have gone on to achieve great things as a player. Despite a good start to his tournament career, he eventually gave up on competitive golf when his religious beliefs prohibited him from playing golf on Sundays.

On one tee shot in that practice round we had to play off a wooden plinth with a mat on it. As I watched Charlie, I noticed that his left heel came off the mat in his back swing and then returned to the mat as he swung the club back to the ball. Not only did it move, but it didn't even come back to its original starting position. Despite all this movement his drive was, as was usual for Charlie, beautifully struck down the middle of the fairway. I watched more closely on subsequent drives and the same movement was repeated every time. We got into quite a discussion about this new discovery and he thought that it helped him achieve the kind of swing I had been encouraging him to develop. "Why don't you try it," he asked?

I hit my best shot of the day and I can still remember the feeling of turning more freely and being more comfortable than I had ever felt at the top of my back swing. It also seemed that I had more impetus when coming back through the ball despite the lack of coil that I had always been indoctrinated to believe as being an essential part of the power process. As usual, although this was significant to me as a player, my thoughts quickly turned to the consequences for the average golfer and how I had been coaching up to that point. I applied this new footwork whenever I saw benefit to a particular player but it was only with a concerted effort to study the effects of free movement during my time at Stoneham Golf Club that my confidence in movement became fully established. The question now was how to persuade people to move more as it seemed that simply telling them to do so was not enough. I needed them to feel the consequences of moving or not moving so that they could choose for themselves. Strange as it may seem, most golfers feel quite comfortable with their awkward swings purely because they have always played that way and don't realise just how uncomfortable they are. They are in a straight jacket created by their false beliefs and just don't know any better. How sad it is that many players never experience a totally relaxed swing but carry on playing all their golf under the impression that they have no natural ability and are simply stiff and uncoordinated.

The technique that I developed to help experienced players is different than coaching total beginners. For someone who has literally never hit a golf ball before, it is only necessary to show him or her that they possess the skill to hit a ball with their eyes shut while moving excessively and then progress to 'La Danse du Golf' with the six basics of a good golf swing. During this process I am still keen for them to understand and feel the consequences of the wrong basics, as I know that normal, though unsolicited, advice will tempt them in the opposite direction. They will probably require information at some stage regarding their grips and basic posture but I will feed these in gradually and very much on the basis of an evaluation of how effective and important these modifications are in each player's individual case.

Traditional teaching would have us believe that a good grip is fundamental and invariably starts with this imperative. I work from the opposite point of view and look at the grip on a 'need-to-know' basis. I prefer to leave established golfers with their comfortable and familiar way of holding the club and, when they are swinging the club with improved rhythm and fluidity and hitting the ball with more confidence, I will turn to their grip if the trajectory and direction requires attention. I can only tell you that my experience shows that this is often not required at all!

When looking at the masterpieces of artists such as Turner, Picasso and Rembrandt can you tell how they were holding their brushes? Does it matter one iota?

In golf it only matters if your way of gripping the club has a consistently negative effect on the way the ball flies. Only then will you need to review your grip.

Trevino, Locke & Sewgolum

I remember watching Lee Trevino practicing for the then Piccadilly World Match Play Championship at Wentworth. His alignment was well to the left of the target, he had a 'strong' or 'hookers' grip, took the club back outside the line, looped it back on the inside and hit the most delightful low fades you've ever seen.

I was fortunate as a youngster to have caddied for, and a year later played with, the famous South African player Bobby Locke at the East Berks. He aimed further to the right than Trevino aimed to the left, had a 'weak' or 'slicers' grip, took the club miles inside on the back swing, came down on the outside of his back swing but, due to his exceptionally closed stance, still well on the inside of the ball to target line, and hit the most amazingly high hooks. Even his pitches moved several yards from right to left in the air.

These two champions had completely opposite methods but both controlled the ball as if it were on a piece of string. They also putted the way they played the full shots and were both wonderful putters. In Bobby Locke's case I doubt that there has ever been anyone better on the greens. He beat Sam Snead twelve times out of fourteen in exhibition matches and, in two and a half years on the American Tour, competed in fifty nine tournaments winning eleven times and finishing in the top three an incredible thirty times. Coming from South Africa, he was not popular in the States and was once interviewed after another winning performance. He was asked about his weak left hand grip, much talked about and criticised by the other pros. "Master," he replied (he called everyone Master), "that's no problem. I take the cheques with my right hand!"

Trevino was a truly great player who had superb rhythm. He won 29 tournaments on the PGA Tour and 2 British Opens, 2 US Opens and 2 USPGA's. He was famous for his sense of humour and incessant talking on the golf course. He once played with Tony Jacklin and was reported to reply to Jacklin's comment about not wishing to talk too much by saying "that's ok, Tony. I can do the talking for both of us!"

"Papwa" Sewsunker Sewgolum was a black South African who played to the very highest level at a time when apartheid was at its height. Sewgolum, a former caddie, with his wrong-way-round grip (left hand beneath his right) caused a stir in 1963 when he beat 103 white golfers including Harold Henning in the provincial Natal Open tournament at the Durban Country Club. He became a symbol of the sports boycott movement when pictures of him receiving his trophy outdoors in the rain, because, due to apartheid, he was not allowed to enter the clubhouse, were published across the world. In 1965 he beat Gary Player to win the title for the second time. He also won the Dutch Open in 1959, 1960 and 1964. He was the winner of a number of non-white golfing championships in South Africa.

Let's imagine that Lee, Bobby and "Papwa" went to have lessons as kids. How easy would it have been to say to all three of them that they must sort out their technical anomalies? "Come on lads, let's get you square to the target line with good grips and correct swing planes." How much damage might have been done? They may well have looked good but would they have been able to achieve the same excellence with methods that weren't faithful to some innate and natural instincts? Later I'll tell you about the hawk and the perfectionist which highlights the short-sightedness of trying to develop a perfect technique.

In modern times, just look at Jim Furyk and you would have to say the same thing. But what a wonderful player he is, although I have heard it said that he has a swing that only his mother loves! I would disagree in that he has great rhythm, balance and coordination and hits the ball both sweetly and with superb control.

So, faced with such a wide variety of 'methods' what can we find that they all respect? What can we find in ALL good golfers?

My major ambition has been to find swing basics that every golf teacher or coach could agree with and, furthermore, that every good golfer's swing reflects. We know that every top player has his own grip, his own posture and his own swing plane characteristics. So, let me repeat the six basics which I believe all good golfers display and upon which you would do well to base your golf:

TURNING – WEIGHT SHIFT – RHYTHM – BALANCE –
COORDINATION – SOUPLESSE

"The most useful piece of learning for the uses of life is to unlearn what isn't true"

—Antisthenes - Greek Philosopher &
  Pupil of Socrates (445-365 BC)

Misconceptions

"Ever since I learnt the importance of the belief system and how it works I haven't met a single golfer who is totally free of misconceptions. Often, golfers suffer from an overload of complicated and confusing information and advice."

Changing Beliefs

BEFORE we go back and look at your answers to the questions I put to you in the introduction, let me give you an example of the negative influence of misconceptions in the domain of putting then you can compare your notes with mine.

I was managing the Golf de Sable-Solesmes, a lovely twenty-seven-hole complex near Le Mans in France, when the club hosted a group of British golfers who were playing a competition over our course. There was a dinner after the practice round and I sat next to a lady who, if my memory doesn't trick me, played off a handicap of around ten or eleven. As the meal progressed she told me of her woes on the putting green. You could tell by her mannerisms that the art of putting had become a bit of a nightmare to her. I decided to ask her a couple of questions to at least see if she was trying to putt in what I have found to be the most effective way or whether she may be suffering from a misconception or two. I started by explaining that every professional circuit keeps statistics which they publish at the end of each season and I asked her what, in her opinion, would be the percentage of putts these players hole from six feet throughout the year.

"Oh!" She said. "It must be about ninety per cent."

Her jaw dropped when I told her it was just fifty and that it was the same every year and on every circuit.

We watch a lot of golf on the television and coverage, particularly in the third and fourth rounds, is focused on the leading players who obviously wouldn't be in contention if they were missing a lot of short putts. We just don't get to see the guys who have been putting badly and miss the cut. They help to keep the statistics low.

I asked her what her average from 6 feet might be taking into account her handicap.

"Oh! I'd say about thirty per cent," she replied.

"So, over the course of a year, you may miss two out of every three from about that distance and maybe one out of three on a good day."

"I suppose you're right," she said.

The short putt is an embarrassment just waiting to happen. Once our minds throw up a negative image of us missing the putt we start to get tense. Suddenly, in the light of future embarrassment, something that we could literally do better with one hand and our eyes closed becomes outrageously difficult. This is exactly why tour players work so hard to keep their minds in the present with nothing but positive images, thoughts and outcomes.

I went on to ask her one or two other questions of a more technical nature, firstly about the line that the putter head should take during the swing and, secondly about wrist and hand action. She told me that she had been taught to putt with stiff wrists and to keep the putter on a straight line throughout the movement. She added that she always tried to keep her head completely still whilst putting.

When I told her that I believed that these ideas were preventing her from putting with natural ability she was again evidently shocked. I explained that the putter must move on a curve and that putting with stiff wrists was likely to introduce too much tension, especially in her hands. The act of trying to keep her head still brought on the conflict of moving whilst not moving. Putting requires even more fluid rhythm than any other part of the game. It also needs your hands to be extremely relaxed so that they can operate with deftness and dexterity. Remember what I said about tension being at the root of all evil and that it steals your feel and robs you of your ability. You will see the negative effects of tension nowhere more drastically than on the putting green.

Later the next day, I was delighted, but not surprised, when she rushed up to me in the clubhouse to tell me that she had putted like a dream and had won the competition.

Alternative Beliefs

So, let me give you my version of what I would say to a complete beginner, as per the questions I asked in the 'Before You Start' section, i.e. 'what would you say to a beginner about......'

THEIR HEAD:

Referring to 'La Danse du Golf,' I would advise that the head should move with the body in a coordinated way throughout the swing. Away from the target on the back swing and then forward towards it on the through swing. Even as you hit the ball your head should not stop, just as in any throwing movement. The human head is relatively heavy and, if it gets into the wrong position, it can have a damaging effect on your balance and on your ability to keep the club near your ideal plane. Additionally, keeping it still and down too long can cause back and neck injuries.

In 'The Search for the Perfect Swing,' a scientific study of the golf swing carried out in the 1960s, the authors Cochrane and Stubbs carried out experiments that showed that average head movement in the top players of the era with a driver was over two inches away from the target on the backswing. Why, forty years later, do most amateur golfers still believe that it should stay immobile?

Just a few weeks ago I came across a video clip of Tiger Woods on the youtube.com website. It shows him hitting shots with a camera on the peak of his cap that points down at the ball. As he swings the club away from the ball his head rotates considerably to his right. Yes, even Tiger moves his head! I have subsequently found one of Ben Hogan swinging with a grid background which shows him doing exactly the same. I don't remember this piece of information in his famous books!

As a kid I learnt that you should 'hit past the chin.' This meant that my right shoulder had to turn through whilst holding my head down literally for as long as possible as I went through the ball, even to the end of the swing. Can you imagine the torsion and resulting difficulty of trying to do these two opposites at one and the same time? I was suppler then and did this so well that I could see down my back soon after the ball was gone. It was undoubtedly a major contributing factor to the back operation I required at the age of forty six.

THEIR EYES:

Now, in terms of the eyes, I am not going to tell beginners to play with them shut, of course. No, I'm going to get them to believe that they can hit it without seeing it so that they develop more belief in their inborn ability and develop more feel for the ball. Generally, I need say nothing about looking at the ball because, in any case, it is unnatural to look at anything else. However, when someone is breaking free from the shackles of watching the ball too closely and keeping their head too still, I may advise them simply to keep the ball within the field of vision during the back swing. I say this because some players enjoy the sense of freedom when de-blocking their heads so much that they move excessively. I do believe that spending some time on the practice range hitting shots with your eyes shut is particularly beneficial. It encourages you to rely more on feel than sight and will increase your self-confidence.

In truth, do we need to tell beginners to keep their eye on the ball? What else would they be looking at? After all, the ball isn't going to suddenly disappear, is it? This advice surely comes from other sports like tennis, cricket and football in which, of course, you play with a moving ball. Over-emphasis on the ball creates tension, which leads to inhibited movement and the feeling of being a prisoner to the ball.

Annika Sorenstam was, apparently, having some difficulty with the way she moved through the shot and her coach asked her to practice letting her head rotate through before she hit the ball. She was looking up before she hit it! A while later, he told her that she didn't need to do it any more as her swing had improved. She had found the new movement so much easier and was hitting the ball so much more comfortably that she decided to stay with it. To this day her eyes and head have already moved forward before the ball is hit. Once you understand that giving your head this freedom also allows you to get your right side, not just your shoulder but literally your whole body through the shot, you will be able to achieve your proper finish position with ease.

THEIR ARMS:

They should be kept as relaxed as possible just as you would if you wanted to throw a ball a long way. Your muscles work best and at their fastest when they are supple and elastic. How many amateurs do you see with hyper tense and rigid arms and shoulders? In this state, how can they possibly develop speed with feel?

Ok, Tiger does it, but you have to ask yourself the question "Am I in the same category of athlete?" I leave you to answer this question yourself. I believe that it was Harvey Pennick who was asked at a US-PGA teaching conference, what he thought about the head still, left arm straight method. "Nothing wrong with it" he said, adding dryly, "as long as it doesn't affect your swing, no, there's nothing wrong with it at all!"

There must be an amount of leeway in any good coach's armoury that allows the individual to display his own way of doing things. In 'La Danse du Golf' I am simply opening your eyes to the potential difficulty that you may have unwittingly added to the way you play the game. Remember, if you can swing the club with a good level of the six basics then I am happy that you 'do your own thing.'

THEIR FRONT FOOT ON THE BACK SWING?

I would strongly advise them to move it freely, especially until they have a good grasp of the 6 basics. I believe that keeping the feet still in the back swing is one of the major factors in most players' awkwardness in the golf swing movement and I am talking especially to those who don't see themselves as natural sports people. In particular, once you get into your forties and fifties I believe that it is pretty much essential. I will go further. Traditional thinking advocates the 'coil' method wherein the shoulders turn against resisting hips and legs with the feet glued to the ground. I believe, on the contrary, that movement should start from the feet as they are the real motors of the golf swing. Jack Nicklaus said as much in his books but failed to go into any further detail. If you have seen him play or seen pictures of him at the top of the back swing with a driver you will have seen just how much his left heel came off the ground.

In another clip on YouTube, I found Ben Hogan demonstrating the importance of good use of knees and hips. He moves very freely and his left heel comes off the ground by the end of his back swing. This is another point I don't remember reading in his 'Modern Fundamentals' but I have studied the drawings which do, indeed, suggest that his heel came off the ground.

THE LINE THE CLUB HEAD TAKES IN THE FIRST FOOT OF THE BACKSWING:

As far as I'm concerned there is no such thing as a straight line in the golf swing other than the one between the ball and the intended target. Trying to keep the club on a straight line will probably produce an upright swing plane and cause the body to slide or sway instead of rotating. I will talk more about this later in 'Why the club doesn't swing on a straight line' when I'll tell you about my brother's discovery and the proof he found for this phenomenon. Please allow me one technical term, 'centrifugal force.' This is the most powerful aspect of a throwing movement and can only be created by a turning motion. When your body fails to turn sufficiently its ability to produce this force is compromised. Thanks for that. I promise not to do it again!

SAME QUESTION REGARDING THE FOLLOW THROUGH:

Same response as Q5 but I would add a bit of interesting information about club face rotation from research done by A.J. Bonar, an American PGA Pro who was consultant technician to the Acushnet Golf Company, makers of the Titleist balls and clubs. "AJ" studied the top players and found that the toe end of the club head moves faster than the heel. To be more precise, the face of the club rotates by up to two-and-a-half degrees per inch. That is to say it is thirty degrees shut by the time it is twelve inches past impact. I have yet to find a golfer who isn't surprised at this statistic. Even if we think that it should close we never knew by just how much. Most of us still think that it is right to keep it pointing to the target for as long as possible. Seems logical, doesn't it? But, of course, if it should be closed for the ball to go straight (remember, the ball has already gone by now) then holding it square is actually holding it open to where it should be. This is the main reason for slicing in golf! It also results in lost distance as the weight of the club head has not been fully released into the shot.

The correct position of the club head a foot after impact is to the left of the ball to target line and the correct orientation of the clubface is considerably left of that.

WHEN IN THE BACKSWING SHOULD YOU COCK THE WRISTS:

Ideally, this action should start at the same time as the club moves away from the ball and continue until the club gets to the top. It's just like using a hammer. You wouldn't think about your wrist action, you'd just swing and hit the nail without any thought of how you were doing it. It's a natural movement but one that many golfers have been persuaded to see as a mechanical affair. I find that women, in particular, have been encouraged to cock their wrists at the end of the back swing. The fact is that a golf club is heavy for a woman and she needs to get early wrist action as it dynamically lightens the club and gives her more impetus and momentum to swing the club back and through the ball with good acceleration. I'm afraid that the 'one piece takeaway' in which the wrists are inactive during the first part of the back swing led many of us in an unnatural and over-mechanical direction as well as leading us to a mistrust of our hands and wrists. Just dwell for a moment on the perverse effect of failing to trust the most marvellous and highly talented inventions, our hands. The 'square-to-square' method that golfers from the 1970's will remember also provoked a less natural and awkward movement. This falsely encouraged many golfers to keep the club face looking at the target for as long as possible on the back swing and again after impact.

WHEN DOES THE CLUB HEAD REACH ITS GREATEST SPEED:

I wonder how many of you will have answered 'at impact?' Well, sorry, the intention has to be after impact and even quite a distance after the ball has gone. Where is the logic in that, you may ask? Surely we need all the speed we can get at the moment the club hits the ball? You are forgetting the fact that an accelerating club head will impart more dynamic impetus to the ball than one with constant speed. Physics wasn't a strong subject of mine at school but I do remember a demonstration of two objects hitting each other on a rail. One was static (i.e. the ball) and the other was moving (i.e. the club head). If the moving object hits the static one at a constant speed it won't project the hit object as far as if it was hit whilst accelerating, even if the speed at impact is the same.

When trying to get maximum speed at impact you are likely to rush your down swing and you will see little reason to finish your movement fully. You cannot stop at the very point where you need to reach your maximum speed so this is especially valid for those players who never seem to get right through to a full finish position. You only need to look at the modern tennis players to see how much speed they generate in the later part of their swings on a forehand drive, long after the ball has been hit.

WHAT SHOULD YOU DO AFTER A BAD SHOT:

This subject needs more attention as it has only a little to do with how you swing the club and a whole lot to do with how you are going to enjoy your game and improve your performance. I'll talk more about this essential topic in 'PART 2: Increasing Your Confidence.' It is fundamental to sustaining improved performance and reducing tension and frustration in your game. My response to the question about what to do after a round of golf will also be found in that section.

"I want to write books that unlock the traffic jam in everybody's head"

—John Updike – American Novelist, Poet and Literary Critic (Born 1932)

My Journey From 'Knowing' To 'Not Knowing'

> "The ability to do something well doesn't require that you know how you're doing it. Too much conscious thought can, in itself, create obstacles to achieving repeatable and sustainable success."

First Day At Work

WHEN I first put pen to paper, or fingertips to the computer pad, to write this book it was 7am on Monday 5th November 2007 and I found myself reflecting on what was happening in my life on this day and at this very hour 40 years before. I have decided that, after 4 decades as a Golf Pro, now was the right time to set my thoughts on paper. Like most golf teachers I have always talked about 'writing my book' but I never really felt comfortable about it and had always found the excuse of a lack of time in order to put it off. I suppose that I was also waiting for the confidence to do it and, now that I am totally convinced about my beliefs, enough to call myself a 'coach' rather than a 'teacher,' there is no reason to put it off any longer.

The 5th November 1967 was not only Guy Fawkes or "Bonfire Night," but it was my first day as the Assistant Pro at the East Berkshire Golf Club. I was just 16 years old and had fallen in love with the game of golf at about the same time that the England football team was winning the World Cup at Wembley in 1966. No, don't worry, passionate as I was about this new game in my life even I watched the football and was not on the golf course on that famous afternoon.

This tall, lanky youngster was, then, full of excitement and expectation on that Sunday morning as he got up, having hardly slept a wink, to start his working life. But, here I must let you into a secret. In all these forty years I've never been to work. I've gone to a golf club every day! I am one of life's lucky people who found a way of making a living from his passion. Oh yes, there have been many days when it has seemed like hard work, especially during the years when I managed golf clubs and found myself squeezed between the directives of the owners and the demands of the members. But all in all, even at those times, I was able to keep perspective on the fact that many, many people have jobs they simply had to do and had no real passion for. Furthermore, I was surrounded by wonderfully manicured greens and fairways in a paradise of beautiful nature, whereas most people find themselves in offices and factories having had to commute in crowded trains and buses to get there. I just had a 50 yard stroll from home to the pro-shop and enough time to smell the pine forest, the heather and the newly mown grass and say 'good morning' to a couple of squirrels.

How sad I am that my father, who had been promoted to Head Office in London and had bought a house so close to a golf course having never played golf in his life, now found himself, at the age of 50, having to commute from this haven of natural beauty into the City spending nearly 4 hours a day travelling. I was undoubtedly the main beneficiary of the move South from Manchester as it gave me the opportunity to discover why I was put in this world and provided me with a way of life that was to underpin my whole existence.

So, here I am, waiting at the door of the little old wooden pro-shop at 8am on that November morning when my new boss, Roger, arrives to open up. In we go and I find myself in the workshop with bits of club here and there, shafts and grips and old persimmon driver heads, and the smell of varnish in the air. I've been here before but as an outsider, just another member of the club and a junior one at that. Now I'm proudly here as part of the pro-shop staff in the inner sanctum of the Club Pro's world. Does it get any better than this for a 16 year old?

Reality begins to set in as my first task is to hoover the carpet and then dust the stock. Funny, isn't it? I never did those things willingly at home. Ah, but this is different. Not only am I as keen as mustard to please my new boss, but also my status in life has just changed and, if dusting is a part of this new world, then so be it. In any case, my mother always told me that it wasn't the type of job you did that is important, but more a question of your own attitude to it and how well you carried it out. I think, at the time, she was trying to persuade me that vacuuming the lounge carpet had some deeper meaning and value. Anyway, I now set about becoming the best cleaner Roger has ever employed.

I am sure that you all remember the experience of your first day in a new job. You feel ill at ease and don't quite know what to do or how to do anything worthwhile. My boss obviously saw that awkwardness in me and knew that he couldn't train me in everything that morning and, when all the cleaning jobs were done at about ten o'clock, he sent me out to practice. Wow! I never expected this. I've only done two hours work and I'm now going to hit balls as part of my job. As I walk across the car park towards the practice ground I had a little internal chat with myself and decided that, from today, I was a professional golfer so handicaps were a thing of the past. "Now, young man, you must play scratch golf," I convinced myself!

Whilst this is an admirable objective, the jump in my case was from being a bandit off ten – not bad after a year's golf - to playing perfect golf with a zero handicap. Of course, this improvement was impossible to achieve in the short walk from the Pro-Shop to the practice ground but what does an enthusiastic sixteen-year-old care about such insignificant obstacles as time and experience? By the time I hit my first shot that day I was, in my mind, already there. After all, I had played a lot of golf by then and had proved that I could hit every shot in the bag and par every hole on the course.

This internal conversation between "I" and "myself" was the beginning of a difficult period in my game. I will be talking to you later about these internal conversations and how powerful they can be, both in a positive and, so often, in a negative sense. Suffice it to say at this stage that the knowledge that we can hit good shots and that 'par' is the ultimate target provides us golfers with all the elements we need to become angry, frustrated and disappointed, and don't we all know what these emotions can do to our games?

So, I have decided to reduce my handicap by ten shots in ten minutes and feel quietly confident in my ability to achieve this as I am now free from all those constraints that have been holding me back like school, homework and exams. I now intend playing some golf every day. I expect to get some expert tuition to help my cause and am delighted when Roger tells me that I have got a lesson on the Monday morning.

"Thanks, I am really looking forward to my lessons with you," I said, gratefully.

"No," he replied, "you're going to give a lesson."

"How can I do that? I've never given a lesson in my life and wouldn't know where to start."

"You'll be alright," he states in a matter-of-fact way. "Your pupil's a young beginner and you know more about golf than he does!"

Doesn't this demonstrate the classic golfing culture? It is your status as a player that counts much more than any specific training or education you have received, or any qualification or skill you have as a teacher. As long as someone has played a little longer than you or plays a little better than you, they will feel quite comfortable about telling you exactly what you're doing wrong. Watch out, you will also feel quite comfortable in taking their advice.

Although I agree that I should have had some guidance before being set free on the unsuspecting public, I do believe that the modern system has become too institutionalised and our young pros are going out to teach with far too much technique in their minds. When I was a PGA Swing Instructor and Examiner in the 1980's I remember that the great theme was to have pros at either end of the country able to give exactly the same advice to the same golfer. Whilst this is an admirable intention I have to tell you that, twenty five years down the line, it has not been achieved.

First Lesson

So, there I am out on the practice ground at the East Berks to give my first golf lesson with little or no idea what I'm going to do or say only to find that he is a left-hander! Not only do I not know what to say, but I also have to reverse every 'right' and 'left.' If you are reading this and are a left-handed golfer who had a lesson with Brian Sparks on Monday 6th November 1967, please accept my sincere apologies. It must have been the worst lesson I ever gave!

As I'm fumbling my way through, I suddenly remember having overheard my predecessor giving a lesson to a beginner a few weeks before and so I repeat the words he had used, 'straight left arm on the back swing, straight right arm in the follow through.' Of course, as a left-hander that got him in quite a pickle until I remembered to reverse the words! As a concept it was also fundamentally flawed but I didn't know that at the time.

What I generally found in those early experiences of teaching was that my pupils didn't look very natural and I was left with an underlying sense that they should be doing better. Somehow, intuition was telling me that they had a good swing within them and it was my duty to help them find it and let it out.

After stumbling my way through those first thirty minutes, and despite the pupil having still paid the six shilling fee, I realised that I needed to find out much more about the golf swing if I was to teach confidently and successfully. Roger generously paid for me to go to the PGA training course for a week in Llandudno the following autumn. I must thank my first boss for opening my young mind to the possibilities that my new-found profession could provide. He is still an active golf pro to this day and has given many youngsters like me the chance to succeed in golf. His enthusiasm and love for the game are exceptional and he was always positive in demonstrating that golf can provide a marvellous way of life and a good living for anyone who has the passion for the game.

I must also thank him for coming round to talk to my father who, having decided my fate as an accountant at a very early age, needed some persuasion to let his eldest son quit school at the age of sixteen leaving his 'A' levels behind, to follow his passion in the unknown world of golf. Let's not forget that this was the 1960's and golf was very much a minor sport and couldn't be considered a solid foundation for a young man's future, especially by my father who had spent his whole working life in the conservative world of banking.

Thirst For Knowledge

After this first attempt at giving a golf lesson I decided to read everything and anything I could get my hands on about the golf swing and I remember spending hours poring over Ben Hogan's famous book The Modern Fundamentals of Golf which seemed to cover just about everything I needed to know. The swing plane represented by a pane of glass was of particular interest to me because I had been ribbed by the previous assistant about my 'beginner's loop,' my 'out-to-in' downswing. I will admit that I hit my drives with a little fade but rarely sliced the ball and was the straightest driver amongst the juniors. That is, until I was told that I had a 'hookers grip,' in other words my hands were too far to the right side of the grip, a typical cricketer's fault (I had been a passionate cricketer until golf took over my life). I absorbed all of Ben Hogan's advice and copied his grip and got the famous 'V's pointing between my chin and right shoulder, as advised. I admit to finding this concept somewhat vague as my 'V's seemed not to be straight lines and they pointed in rather indiscriminate directions.

A hooker's, or 'strong,' grip where the hands are placed more to the right side of the shaft for a right-handed player should produce a shot that goes to the left but my drives had always drifted a little to the right. It was predictable and allowed me to know how to get the ball on the fairway. Remember my comments about Lee Trevino's swing and grip? He had a hooker's grip but hit the ball exactly where he wanted to with the ball moving slightly to the right, in fact it was a beautiful fade. But I still didn't know enough about golf at that time and it didn't register until many years later that he was disproving the basic principles of the knowledge I was gaining. As Gary Player once said, "for every fundamental in golf I'll show you a superstar, and I don't use the word lightly, who doesn't do it."

Now that I had a neutral, or weaker, grip that prevented the clubface from closing I began to present an open clubface to the ball which caused a big slice. "That's normal at the start," I was told, "but the slice will disappear if you practice enough." Well, I just loved hitting balls so off I went with my new grip with the intention that, if it was just a question of hitting a few thousand balls, then I'd do that in a few days. After all, practice makes perfect, we all know that. Unfortunately, this old proverb is flawed because in reality practice makes permanent. I can still remember my new grip being so uncomfortable. It gave me the feeling of having the wrong hand on the wrong arm as well as giving me a load of blisters.

Armed with my new nearly permanent slice I began to find the game difficult for the first time especially as the East Berks course is quite narrow with thick heather and pine forests lining the fairways. Before I took up golf, cricket had been my passion in life and I was an opening batsman who showed some promise. With a cricket bat in my hand the basics were simple; keep the bat straight, hit down the line and keep your eye on the ball. To hit it to the left I just turned the bat to the left and vice-versa if I wanted it to go to the right. But I didn't want to hit the ball to the right or left on the golf course. This is where the game of golf is so more exacting than most other sports as we nearly always want to hit it straight down the middle off the tee and then straight onto the green with our approach. In cricket and tennis the player is actually trying to deceive his opponent by hitting the ball in unexpected directions. Some of their greatest shots may even come from unintentionally wayward shots, rarely an attribute in golf.

After a year of golf you could say that I "knew" how to play. It was relatively uncomplicated and natural to me. A couple of years down the line I had gained an enormous amount of knowledge and had, so it seemed, drastically improved my swing technique. I had hit thousands and thousands of balls, had had a club in my hands for several hours every day (yes, even Christmas day) and, do you know what? I could no longer break eighty, something that I had been doing regularly in my first year. I had gone from hitting most fairways to missing most of them and was now getting very frustrated about my game. Armed with all of this new knowledge you could even say that I didn't "know" how to play anymore!

> "In your search for knowledge be sure not to drown in all the information."
>
> —Anthony J. D'Angelo - Chief Visionary Officer at Collegiate Empowerment USA

Conforming to Traditional Technique

"Too late, I realise that the 'late hit' often made me miss out on hitting the ball at the right time"

The Late Or Lagged Hit

A major part of my slide into mechanical golf happened one morning the following summer. My boss duly saw that I was again 'in the way' and sent me out to play a few holes on my own.

What a glorious morning! The sun is shining on the flowering heather, the aroma of the pine forest is at its most perfumed best and, as on most summer days on a golf course, there is the smell of newly mown grass in the air. This heavenly state is even more poignant to this seventeen-year-old as he knows that all his friends are locked away in a classroom at the Forest Grammar School being force-fed on 'A' Level French, Economics and English.

You know, it's a strange thing but I have never been able to play well on my own. With every shot that isn't struck to perfection I take the opportunity to play another ball whilst searching for the technical error on the previous shot. Soon, I have so many balls in play that I forget which one I hit first and seem to lose all sense of scoring. My head spins with a myriad of possible faults crowding my mind. Of course, I am getting deep into the 'paralysis by analysis' syndrome but am totally unaware of the phenomenon. My motivation disintegrates and I get a bit grumpy with myself. I try to limit myself to two balls, playing one against the other, but this fails to rectify my problems as I know from the outset that I will both win and lose. Over the years, I have come to recognise motivation as one of the most powerful assets in achieving goals and you must never underestimate it.

I decide to play the last three-hole loop and have just teed off on the eighteenth when I met Stan, the amiable Head Green Keeper, a four-handicap golfer who came to East Berks from Sunningdale. In one or two earlier conversations he had displayed knowledge of golf that had this youngster wide-eyed in admiration. Golf was, at that time, held up as a bastion of snobbery. I was the only golfer at my school of over seven hundred pupils and had even suffered some bullying because I played golf. A club like Sunningdale was full of 'toffs' and 'gentry' but they had a thriving artisan section which was made up of ordinary people who paid low fees for limited playing rights in return for some work on the course. Some of them, according to Stan, were marvellous golfers and wonderfully colourful characters who had been scratch or better for more years than he could remember.

To say that I am in awe of this knowledgeable man is an understatement. I hang on his every word and on this particular morning he seems to have spare time on his hands and so proceeds to describe and demonstrate the intricacies of the golf swing in minute detail. There is much for this youngster to take in but here is what I remember:

Backswing: feet, hips and head still whilst turning shoulders as far as possible so as to create the coil effect, like winding up a spring

Downswing: start by moving the left hip towards the target and transferring your weight to the left foot, pulling the club down vertically as if it's a bell rope

Hitting area: hold back your wrists until the latest possible moment then release the club with hands and wrists with maximum acceleration whilst hitting against a firm left leg and getting your right shoulder to hit under your chin. Keep looking at the point where the ball had been

Follow through: keep your head down for as long as possible while extending your arms as far as you can down the line toward the target

Finish: hands as high as possible

Not only do I hear all this wonderful advice, but also he demonstrates every stage of the movement to me in slow motion, position by position. The words have maybe got lost over the years but the images of his swing are still with me forty years later.

He finishes his demonstration by stressing these words: "Brian, the 'late hit' is the one thing that distinguishes the great golfers from the others. Now that you have the time, go and work on this until you've got it, however much practice it might take and however much your hands blister and bleed in the process. It'll be worth it."

Well, what else could I do but make for the practice ground to work on the 'secret of golf.' Over the ensuing months I learnt to release the club later and later and, whilst I could occasionally rescue the situation by whipping the club into the ball at the eleventh hour with my irons, I started to present an ever increasingly open face to the ball with the driver. My gentle fade, which had already turned into a bit of a slice, had now turned into a confidence shattering block slice. The ball started out over the rough on the right and curved further away as it invariably fell into the trees. No longer did I threaten the middle of the East Berks fairways but put the fear of God into the squirrels that had, up until then, enjoyed a relatively peaceful life in the dense dark depths of the pine forests! With my driver put into early retirement even my three-wood was beginning to catch the same disease.

Stan passed away many years ago and I must stress that I retain no feeling of malice towards him. After all, I know that any one of a thousand golfers of that era could, and would, have given me the same advice. That was the way golf mechanics were viewed at that time. The fact is that he was a lovely man who saw something in me and just wanted to help. It is worth noting that he was a good player despite his thoughts on the golf swing. He may well have been capable of playing to a much higher standard if his technique had been simplified. The plain truth is that everyone played like that at the time and, however much difficulty there may be in any way of swinging a golf club, there will always be those who are the best and those who play less well.

Becoming A Tour Player

In 1971 my father met a wealthy English entrepreneur and an American colleague of his for lunch in London. After the business was concluded and, knowing my father, with a brandy and cigar in hand, the conversation turned to more personal matters and the three men talked about their families. My father proudly talked about his two wonderful daughters and their new husbands, a doctor and a flour miller, and the excellent school reports of his youngest son who would, no doubt, go on to university. He finished by shyly admitting that his eldest son was a professional golfer.

"Oh," said the American, "one of my companies sponsors a Golf Pro in the States. It's been a wonderful thing to do."

My surprised father warmed to the subject and told them a lot more about me. The Englishman showed some interest in the idea of copying his friend and duly asked my father to send me to meet him at his country estate in Eastbourne the following week and to bring my clubs.

When I arrived at his home I was taken to the Royal Eastbourne club where it had been arranged for me to play with the American's wife as she was a good golfer whereas the two men were not even regular players. (My would-be sponsor played with one of those adjustable clubs and a pocketful of balls.) Despite being extremely nervous and topping my first tee shot in front of them all, I improved as the round progressed and the lady reported that I played good golf and I was duly sponsored for three years on the professional circuit. How bad is this? Four years ago a schoolboy, now a world traveller on the tournament scene and I haven't reached twenty yet!

Roger had always held the opinion that, at the age of fifteen, I had started to play too late to contemplate making it as a tour player so I didn't ask his advice on my sponsorship deal. As a new recruit to the tournament player's ranks I didn't seek his help, or anyone else's for that matter. How naive I was not to have asked more of him or even to ask my sponsor to provide me with some top coaching. Looking back, money had not been a problem. I had been asked to say what I needed and had been given no indication that there was a financial limit. The simple facts are that I was too shy to ask for more than £2,000 per annum and I had no idea at that time that I needed so much help to learn how to tap into my natural talent and ability.

There have been many examples of people starting to play golf much later than me and still reaching the top. Greg Norman only started to play golf when he was sixteen and Calvin Peete, a black American with a deformed left arm, started in his twenties and not only became the straightest driver on the American circuit, but also went on to play Ryder Cup golf and become one of the world's top ten players.

All I needed, in hindsight, was to be encouraged to believe in my ability to improve. My dream was just that, a dream, but I only needed a few stepping stones or more immediate targets to get me up the first few rungs of the ladder. I have witnessed at first hand just what people can achieve with a little bit of encouragement and a progressive attitude to their possibilities. The truth is that, as coaches or teachers, we pass on to our pupils our inner most beliefs about how good they can become. I simply didn't have that kind of positive influence around me except maybe my sister Pat who did once say to the rest of the family, during the debate as to whether I should be allowed to leave school for a career in golf, "Why shouldn't he become a great golfer?"

Unfortunately, she knew nothing about golf and, when all was said and done, she was my older sister. Young teenage boys don't always listen to older sisters even when they are being defended by them!

My first tournament was at the Mufilira Club in Zambia on the Safari Circuit and I well remember carding an eighty three in the first round with twenty seven putts. This was typical of my game at that time whereby I spent most of the round looking for my ball in the trees on the right and the rest of the time scrambling heroically to break ninety!

I did improve over the first two seasons but only to the extent that I wasn't finishing last anymore. The top of the leader board seemed so far away that I could see no great future and was getting increasingly depressed by it all. So, I decided to give up my sponsorship with a year left to go. Maybe I am being a bit hard on myself as I did get a lot better and had put in a few good rounds but I couldn't see it at the time. Golf just doesn't encourage us to take the positives out of what we're doing. 'Au contraire,' it seems designed to do the very opposite as we are all in search of the Holy Grail of consistency. Of course, it is virtually impossible, however good a player you are, to play even nine holes without a bad shot.

When asked how they have played today, how many golfers do you hear respond in a positive manner? Instead of telling you about the few really good shots they hit they will invariably tell you about all the disasters. If you are a negative-pessimist kind of character who has a tendency towards being obsessive-perfectionist, then you will be in for a self-imposed hard time. I am reminded of the golfer who was asked how he had just played. "Oh, not as well as I can do," he replied. "But there again, I never do!"

Back To Being A Club Pro

I went back to being an assistant pro with Roger who had now moved to the new Downshire public course near Bracknell. One year later and I had been appointed to my first full club professional's post at Barton-on-Sea Golf Club in the New Forest near Bournemouth.

When I was interviewed for the job I was twenty-three years old and the Club Secretary informed me that eighty-six per cent of the members were retired. During the interview the Club Captain asked how I got on with older people. I stated that I got on famously with my grandparents. My comment prompted a chuckle from the interviewing committee and probably got me the job.

Once I began to teach at Barton, the members were continually saying 'of course, I can't turn like I used to.' Unfortunately, at that time, I only knew what I had been taught which was to keep the feet firmly on the ground on the backswing with the head completely still so I wasn't able to help them as much as I could have done. As I said earlier, I was also encouraged as a youngster to turn my shoulders against my hips, as it would apparently produce a powerful coil effect. In reality, it made a good swing more difficult for me and is one of the reasons why I ended up with a serious back injury that required surgery when I was in my forties. I leave it to your imagination as to what this way of playing can do to players in their sixties and seventies. 'La Danse du Golf' will reveal just how easy it would have been to get those members to turn more, just as I have done so many times now, none, I must admit, with more success than with Henry, a retired policeman from Broadstairs in Kent, who has reduced his handicap from fifteen to twelve in the last 12 months at the age of seventy seven!

In 1975 I bought my first portable video system and I began to see some rather strange images, especially as golfers went through the hitting area. I just had to ask myself why people were doing such strange things with a golf club, such as getting so cramped for space at impact. So many golfers got in their own way that it was no surprise that their shots were often less than satisfactory. Ever since I gave that first lesson to the young left-hander and began to look at how golfers swing a golf club with a critical eye I had been amazed at how awkward many of them looked. I had an innate vision of how simple it should be and, even if I was struggling myself, I was always keen to work on simple basics when teaching.

The most revealing fault that I saw repeated time and time again was the lateness of the hit. Now, I'm not talking about a 'late hit' in terms of the classic late release of the wrists at impact as described to me by Stan. No, I'm more concerned to see such late and awkward effort just to get the club back to the ball. Most people just made it look impossibly difficult. So much so, in fact, that their whole body would deform into a mass of tension that showed as their faces screwed up with lips tightly pursed, teeth painfully gritted and the type of frowns usually reserved for the most difficult arithmetic problems or the world's worst case of toothache. The amount of physical input was invariably out of all proportion to the output in terms of how well or how far the ball was hit. The player's weight would usually stay on the back foot which would be firmly glued to the ground until the short, stabbing follow through came to its abrupt finish. All in all, not a pretty sight!

Compare this with what I saw when studying good players and the situation was completely reversed. I couldn't fail to be impressed by the likes of Tom Weiskopf, Ed Snead, Al Geiberger and Hale Irwin. There is no better example of this in today's game than Annika Sorenstam who makes every part of her movement look totally relaxed and natural. Have a look at her excellent book 'Golf - Annika's Way' and you will see someone completely at ease with the golf swing in every picture. She looks as if she is doing something easy, even making it look like child's play. No gnashing of the teeth here, just an optimum use of the elasticity and efficiency of relaxed muscles and the purity of rhythm, coordination and balance that comes with this style of movement.

Now, here's a fundamental contradiction. I used the word 'movement.' "But, hold on there," I hear you protest, "how do you move and, at one and the same time, not move your head, feet and spine?" The golf teacher's classic response is to explain that you need to practice for hours and hours and really 'work hard' on this conundrum as it will all come right with time and patience. My reply is very simple but far from the traditional one. Let me answer your question with another. How can you turn your body in the back swing and transfer your weight to the back foot, as everyone agrees that golfers should, whilst keeping your head still and your spine in its original central position? The simple truth is that it is physically impossible and will cause many of the faults that your teacher and well-wishing friends will criticise you for such as "You're not completing your shoulder turn!" "You're not getting your weight through to the front foot!" "You're too stiff." "Relax!"

Golf coaches must recognise that they are teachers of movement and should study the intricacies of the dynamics of movement before subjecting their unsuspecting clients to the sort of physical puzzle more suited to the suppleness of a cat than that of our average golfer.

Can you throw a ball very far whilst standing still? Of course, you can't. So why have you been trying to play this game with your head and feet still for so long?

Annika doesn't keep her head down at impact; she isn't even looking at the ball by then. Her head has turned through before she hits it! Paul Azinger, David Duval, Robert Allenby and Henrik Stenson all do the same to some extent. How can this be? And still today on every golf course in the world you'll hear this excuse for many bad shots; "You lifted your head!"

A perfectionist came across an injured hawk huddling for safety in a doorway. He picked it up and examined it.

"Oh dear, you poor thing," he exclaimed. "What sort of a bird are you? You're not quite right."

He took a pair of scissors and removed the ugly curve in its upper beak so it sat neat and even on top of the lower one. Then he clipped and trimmed its swept-back wings so they were straight. Finally he took his nail clippers to the hawk's talons and cut them right back to the toes.

"There," he said, admiring his handiwork. "Now you look much more like a bird ought to look."

Primary source: Sandra Maitri.
General source: Sufi tradition

Where do our natural abilities go when we play golf?

"If golf teaching has improved so much in the last 40 years why do so many golfers share a belief in out-dated and complicated swing mechanics which block their potential?"

Recognising Good Golfers

COME with me for a moment and use your imagination. Let's watch some golfers as they arrive at a golf club. As they park their cars and take their clubs from their boots, can we spot the good players? Ah, the tall, athletic guy who's pulled up in a smart new silver grey Jaguar must play well. Just look at the cut of his clothes and the size of that bag. Looks like a new set of Mizuno blades. Yes, watch how relaxed he looks as he chats effortlessly with the people around him. He seems well coordinated, hasn't dropped anything, didn't hit another car as he parked and has managed to put his electric trolley together as if it was child's play.

Now, here comes a typical 28 handicapper. Look at his lack of dress sense and that old bag of 1980s clubs, rather matching the old and dirty car he drives. He's a little older than the first chap and certainly couldn't be classed as an athlete unless developing his paunch falls into the arena of regular exercise. Mind you, despite his portly girth and slightly stiff gait, he too seems well coordinated, hasn't dropped anything and walks to the clubhouse with good balance and rhythm in his step. He looks to be a confident type of person as he meets and greets his fellow members.

Can we tell who plays the best golf and who has the best handicap? No, we can't. It could be either of them. So, let's go to the first tee and see if we can get any more clues.

As luck would have it the two men are playing together. The tall, athletic guy has a reasonably good practice swing although he doesn't ooze the same level of confidence that we anticipated after seeing him in the car park. His tee shot is a minor disaster as his backswing only goes half way and his follow through is virtually non-existent as he ends up with his weight firmly stuck on his back foot. There are a few expletives that shroud the air as he hits a good three inches behind the ball. He protests that he had played so well yesterday before shyly retreating to put his latest jumbo-sized titanium all singing, all dancing driver back in the bag, his head held embarrassingly low.

Our second contestant now takes centre stage. As he walks onto the tee there seems to be a near-swagger of authority and his practice swing is amazingly simple and smooth. Giving the impression that golf is purely child's play, the ball is struck with a masterful 'crack' as he creams the most beautiful shot 280 yards straight down the middle. He is still holding a perfectly balanced and composed finish position as his playing partners congratulate him on a splendid drive. He looks a little abashed as he places his old faithful driver back in the tattered and worn bag that we had seen when he arrived.

In reality, we have all seen this at first hand. Unfortunately, the percentage of players who experience the first chap's disaster is extremely high whilst the number of golfers who play like the second fellow is disappointingly low. Why should this be so? Why do so many normal people have so much trouble swinging a golf club? Why does their natural sense of rhythm, balance and coordination, used so well in virtually all other daily tasks, evaporate into thin air as soon as they get a golf club in their hands?

Why has the average handicap not improved in the last 20 years, especially considering the huge improvement in equipment during the same period? Why do people who have been good at all other sports have so much difficulty with golf? Why do women who dance well have such inability to perform the golf swing with the same degree of balance, rhythm and elegance? It just isn't logical!

The 3 'Deadly Don'ts

This question has been nagging away at me for years. In fact, I think it was there from the moment I felt responsible for how my pupils were playing the game. In other words, it had been there since I turned pro. I feel that I had an innate sense of how well they could swing the club and, despite not having the knowledge to back it up, I somehow got through to most people to the extent that anyone taking lessons with me for any length of time seemed to develop an easier and more 'pleasing to the eye' way of swinging. Over the years I have been criticised for what I coach but no one has been able to criticise the way my pupils play.

85

Let me tell you that I have been questioning golfers for well over twenty years about what they see as the main basics of the golf swing. I don't lead the question towards any intended response but ask an open question as to how they would teach a beginner. Most people start by saying that they wouldn't know how to go about teaching someone else as they are having enough difficulty themselves. Interestingly, if this were truly the case we wouldn't have so much poor and unsolicited advice in the game.

There are two groups of response. The vast majority believe that you should 1) keep your head still, 2) keep your leading arm straight and 3) keep the front foot firmly rooted to the ground in the backswing. I would say that fifty per cent believe in all three, seventy five per cent believe in two and ninety per cent believe in at least one of them. A strange fact is that those who don't believe in these things, i.e. the second group, tend to be the better players, although even they still tend to believe in 2) and 3).

Earlier, I told you that I would explain why top golfers have improved their swings and their scores so much whilst the average golfer hasn't. Firstly, they will have developed more confidence in their personal way of swinging and will be less influenced by free advice. Secondly, and most importantly, they will not believe in keeping their heads still. In fact, they probably never think about their heads at all other than realising that their ability to get through the shot will be impaired if their head stays down too long.

Over the years I have added to this list of the '3 Deadly Don'ts' and I now have a list of over sixty widely held misconceptions about the golf swing and how to hit the different shots and how to play the game in general.

Effectively, most of us don't really know what we think and it takes a while to form our thoughts on these matters. Most people reply that they "don't really know." The simple fact is that we don't think about them because they are pre-conceived ideas. They are no longer in our conscious mind as they have been long condemned to the dark waters of the subconscious. Of course, this is where they can be at their most damaging because their voice is not loud enough to penetrate the conscious mind which is too involved with the number of active instructions it is giving you before, and sometimes during, every shot. Beliefs are what our subconscious is trying to conform to. This is the level on which a good coach works and it is only when the erroneous belief is understood at its deepest level that real and lasting improvement will take place. This is where coaching can be at its most effective and can also provide amazingly fast results. I will tell you later about Raymond and the 'quick therapist' story which will expand on this theme.

What Do You Believe

Let us return to the request I made in my introduction to write down your thoughts and then answer my questions. Some of your thoughts no doubt, came easily and some took a little time to come through. Now, re-read your comments. This is not a quiz; there are no rewards to getting it right. In fact, there is no right and wrong only what works best for you. This is simply just a bit more information to give you new options to base your future beliefs on.

According to research, up to ninety five per cent of our actions are controlled by our subconscious minds. In his excellent book Life's a Game So Fix the Odds, Philip Hesketh likens it to riding a wild horse with only five per cent control in your hands. Maybe in golf we fail to recognise this phenomenon and continue to believe that conscious control will do the job, grasping the reins, i.e. gripping the club, more and more tightly. This also explains why we never quite seem to progress in golf in the same way as say driving a car. Both are similar in the early stages but golf seems to require continual attention to an endless list of small matters whilst, with minimal experience, we drive a car with little or no conscious thought. If the truth be known, we probably drive at our best in a sort of 'automatic pilot' state when we aren't thinking at all! Scary, isn't it? Of course, when in this state, we are able to respond immediately to any occurrence and may even react more quickly because there is no conscious thought getting in the way. (Please don't take this as a replacement for the normal requirements of attention and concentration whilst driving.)

The desire to play with maximum control is what leads us to believe in the strictness of keeping things so still and tight and straight. It feels safe to swing this way. It feels that less will go wrong when we grip the club with white-knuckled tension. The fact is that we now see the golf swing as being complex and technical so it is obvious to us all that we need complex and technical solutions. Answer these simple questions:

- Will you let yourself relax and move more freely in a friendly game or in a competition with a card in your hand?
- Will you move more or less when faced with a difficult shot on the last hole of a competition you feel you are just about to win?
- Do you move more freely when you're confident or when you're having a bad time?

'La Danse du Golf' will give you a feel of the correct movement. Feel is the body's language. It is what Jack Nicklaus thought to be the essential element that all top sportsmen and sportswomen resort to when under pressure, not technique. This basic exercise will also increase your awareness of when you stop moving freely.

When I was struggling with my own game the last thing I thought to do was to go back to a natural, thought-free way of playing. I didn't think for a moment that I had learnt my faults. I was too busy practicing to achieve these wonderful new techniques that promised to bring my game to the highest level. When they didn't work I didn't criticise the advice. I criticised myself!

I must distinguish here between beginners and experienced players. Someone who has never played before will have none, or very few, of these erroneous beliefs. This provides a real opportunity to coach in a pure manner, i.e. to allow someone to develop in the most natural and pure way. Careful though. We coaches must not think that this is an occasion to show off all our knowledge.

Keep It Simple

Remember, a good coach is centred on his client and not himself. I have long believed that there are two types of teacher; teacher-centred and pupil-centred. I once witnessed a well-known pro giving a clinic to a dozen novices. It took forty minutes for him to describe the intricacies of the golf swing before they even got their hands on a club. By this time you could see the boredom on their faces and the confusion in their eyes as they struggled with the expert terminology.

I believe that the greatest teachers communicate their knowledge in the simplest ways. Evidently, many experts hide behind their technical expertise by using complicated words and jargon which is all very impressive but of no use in a coaching environment. As Martin H Fischer (American physician and author) once said, *"You must learn to talk clearly. The jargon of scientific terminology which rolls off your tongues is mental garbage."*

Why don't we just ask a beginner to show us how she would do it naturally? If we take this approach we might just find that we have a pure, natural talent before us who does everything we thought we had to teach her. Over-coaching is responsible, in my opinion, for the lack of progress in recent years. But, also, coaching has become too technical with the advent of video playback facilities whereby the coach can compare your swing with that of a tour pro with whom you haven't got anything in common, be it athletic build, hours on the practice ground or the fact that he or she has been playing every day for the last fifteen years.

I do use video when it is necessary and it can be of enormous help, but I agree with Butch Harmon who recently said that he and his brothers had used it too much and now rely on it to a much lesser degree.

I love the following quote from one of the masters of golf coaching. He knew what a simple thing it is to swing a golf club. Seventy years after his book was published the average golfer still thinks that it's one of the most difficult things he does in his or her life. 'La Danse du Golf' confirms Jones' thoughts on just how easy it really is.

> "It sounds so simple, and it is simple. So simple, in fact, that I find it difficult at times to get pupils to actually accept it."
>
> —Ernest Jones in Swing the Club Head
>   - 1937

Why the club doesn't swing on a straight line

"Our talents and our abilities often lie hidden and under-utilised behind all manner of false but powerful beliefs."

Does The Club Move In Straight Lines Or Curves?

MY life as the Club Pro at Barton-on-Sea had become very comfortable. I had married a New Forest girl, Caroline, and I was enjoying success as a teacher whilst my shop was also providing me with a reasonable income. My young brother, Philip, had become my assistant when he turned pro in 1974 and, together with my other assistants, we spent many hours poring over golf magazine articles and discussing the golf swing. I remember the confusion over quite a few of the articles that went into great technical detail. Quite simply, we couldn't understand some of them, and we were pros!

I bought my first portable video system in 1975 and this gave me new abilities to study golfers' swings in slow motion and even 'frame by frame' and produced some very interesting information. It soon became obvious that the guys writing those magazine articles didn't have the same real images on which to base their thoughts. The written word is a powerful tool but I now had pictures jumping out at me from the video screen that defied much of the logic that I had been fed on up to that time.

In my own game, however, video gave me more insight into the errors in my technique and I worked hard on making yet more improvements. Over a long period of time I could see the benefits as my swing looked better and better. Did my scores improve? Not one iota! I would regularly step on the first tee with great optimism given by the pictures I was seeing of my swing and with a precise set of swing thoughts firmly grooved by hours of hitting balls on the practice ground. After a disappointing or disastrous front nine I would stand on the tenth tee and say to myself 'damn it, you may as well play with no thought at all as it can't get any worse.' I would often produce a back nine close to or below par. The fact that I continued this process with unnerving regularity could seriously call into doubt my intelligence and sanity. But hey, I'm a golfer as much as anyone else. The fact that I call myself a 'pro' doesn't change the nature of the game I'm playing nor the way my emotions work.

What I didn't know at that time was that practice doesn't necessarily make perfect. What it does is make permanent. I was wrongly expecting to find a solution in a technical sense and I was compounding the problem by taking too much conscious thought out onto the golf course. The real value of practice, i.e. repetition, is to not have to think when you are performing, just like a ballet dancer who will spend an inordinate number of hours practicing one movement all day in front of the mirror so that it will happen unconsciously on stage that evening.

I recently coached a pro that was suffering first tee nerves. Things had got so bad that he could hardly get the club moving on his drive off the first tee. He had been working hard on his technique and told me that he was 'nearly there' in terms of how he wanted to swing the club. When I watched him hit shots he took a long time fiddling over the ball and I could sense the amount of thought going on in his head. Honestly, I thought he was never going to hit it. When I asked him what he was thinking about he admitted that he had around twenty swing thoughts! He felt that he only needed one or two more things to reach his goal. Unfortunately, the more he added the worse he got. He was working in completely the wrong direction. I asked him to hit the ball with no thought whatsoever and his swing improved out of all recognition in minutes. My brother had worked with this pro and knew his swing very well. He watched our session and couldn't believe the transformation.

Philip was not the natural golfer of the two of us. He turned pro with a handicap of twenty and had to work his butt off just to pass the playing qualifications to get his PGA badge. At one understandable stage he got frustrated working for his brother and went to work for another pro in Buckinghamshire. We had had some heated words about swing technique and he wouldn't agree that the club must move in a curve around the body and thus leave the ball to target line soon after the start of the takeaway and again soon after impact. Even in those days I believed that the club head should move along a curve (in-to-square-to-in) and couldn't move on a straight line. Philip, on the other hand, believed that it must travel along a straight line for as long as possible if the ball was to go consistently straight to the target. His new boss was a devotee of the straight-line method and Philip was delighted with his new teacher. After all, it wasn't his big brother!

He would regularly come back to see me mainly to show off his 'new' swing. Always a positive character, he would explain just where his new method was so much better than what he had been learning from me and how well he was now playing. Whenever I watched him play or practice he looked worse and worse. But how can you tell that to your kid brother, who is so upbeat about his new swing? Well, I decided that discretion was the order of the day and said nothing until the day he arrived sheepishly requesting that I go out and watch him because things weren't going so well and he wasn't sure that he was on the right track.

After just a few shots it was evident that he was in a right pickle. I knew that I couldn't say much as it would come across as 'older brother' being negative so I got the video out and showed him his swing. I asked him what he thought. I can't use his exact words if I ever want to get this book published but let's just say that he was horrified. He had always had a very upright backswing and lacked natural rotation in his swing. His hips slid instead of turning and he would chop down on the ball. He had been working on keeping the club even more on a straight line both back and through which was producing more lateral action. The balls were going nowhere near the target even with a seven iron in his hands. He went away with a better understanding of his problems and a few questions in his mind about the way he was being taught by his new boss.

A few weeks later he resigned and came back to work for me. One morning, a few months later, he arrived at work and immediately announced that he knew that I had been right about the curved swing path and, what was more, he could prove it. He had built a wooden plinth and attached an old forty-five rpm record which sat at an angle to the base supported by some wire. The disc represented the swing plane. With two more lengths of wire he had attached two beads to represent the golfers' eyes which were out in front of the disc and sitting above it. He asked me to hold the disc horizontally in front of my eyes and, from this position, all I could see was a straight line formed by its edge. When he asked me to angle it towards me by a few degrees so that I could see the record label the disc went from being a straight line to an oval shape and the rim furthest from me went from being a straight line to becoming a curve.

How about this? My brother is not only eating a large slice of humble pie here but he's also proving why I had been right all along! Your eyes are above the plane. Yes, it's as simple as that. Think of a croquet mallet. You stand astride the line you want to hit down and swing the mallet along this straight line because the shaft is vertical to the ground with your eyes directly over the line. In golf, the shaft is at an angle to the ground and your eyes are far from being over the ball. The longer the club, the further your eyes will be on your side of the ball and the more rounded becomes the curve. The roundest swing of all is made with your longest club, the driver. In my opinion, the idea of swinging a golf club on a straight line is one of the main reasons for poor and unnatural golf.

And don't forget that a putter is also not made like a croquet mallet. Sam Snead famously pioneered a method where you stood facing the hole with the ball in between your feet that were placed either side of the ball just like playing croquet, in fact. The 'powers that be' obviously thought that this was making putting too easy (??!!) and banned it. There is now a rule that the shaft has to be at least ten degrees from the vertical so, even in putting, the club should follow a slight curve. You can throw away all those putting trainers that force you to swing too straight! I have had players and pros that challenge this belief but when asked if they would swing the club on a straight line on an eighty-foot putt, they answer that of course they wouldn't. It has to be a curve; otherwise the discomfort at the end of the backswing would be unacceptable. OK then, if that's the case, at what length of putt do you suggest changing from a straight line to a curve? They can't answer that question.

Trusting Technique Or Trusting Yourself

We golfers are always searching for 'the secret' of golf and often come up with some fantastic innovations. I leave it to your imagination just how many I have seen come and go in the last 40 years. I am reminded of the day that Roy, a 14 handicapper at East Berks, arrived for the daily roll-up announcing that he had found the 'secret' of putting. We eventually persuaded him to tell us about this momentous discovery before his round. He explained that he started by pacing the length of the putt and retracing his steps to check his count. He would then lift the putter a certain height calculated on the speed of the green that day and just let the weight of the putter do the rest. He began to doubt the wisdom of letting us in on his secret when it was met with no mean measure of jocular cynicism. As luck would have it, I was drawn to play in a four-ball with him and Roger, the club pro. On the second green, Roy had a putt of about eighteen yards. Roy asked Roger to tend the flag. He duly walked the length of the putt and, when he turned to walk back to the ball Roger, always the joker, took the flag from the hole and walked it three paces nearer to Roy's ball without him noticing. Roy did his measuring with all the due diligence of a quantity surveyor whilst Roger stood expressionless with the flagpole in hand. Needless to say, Roy stood over the ball, had a last glance at his target and then knocked his putt very close to the flag. In all fairness to him, he joined in heartily with our fit of hysterical laughter as soon as he realised that he had been 'had.'

As Dr Joseph Parent says in 'Zen Golf,' *"the intuitive mind is what gets control. It's the expert at running the body and it exerts beautiful control over the tiniest muscle movements if it is not interfered with by the thinking mind."*

As golfers, we are easily persuaded to follow some hare-brained ideas which appeal to our 'thinking minds' because we are always looking for more control or looking to create a faultless and foolproof 'method' so that bad golf and bad shots are eradicated from our games. The more we go down this road the more we comfort ourselves that we are doing the right thing. It's a bit like the 'work ethic' of the nineteenth century in that it was thought that lots of analysis and hard work can't fail. How many of you have experienced that feeling of coming away from a golf lesson with your head full of new, complicated and un-natural techniques? Can this explain why so many players don't take lessons? Have our teaching techniques frightened you off? I, for one, wouldn't be at all surprised.

A good coach will leave you feeling uplifted, liberated and gener-ally excited about how easy it has been to hit the ball well; how easy it has been to play effortless and natural golf because the plain truth is that he has only enabled you to do something that you were already more than capable of. He or she won't tell you too much in one session, as this is self-defeating. Hank Haney, Tiger's current coach, advises us to say less when we coach and goes on to say that he finds it difficult to persuade even the coaches at his own academy to talk less!

I remember Arthur, at the age of 75 and with 40 years golf behind him, thanking me for being the first person to have ever given him a

97

golf swing. He said that I was the only coach to have done this after many lessons with many different pros over the years. I was touched by his words but politely refuted them by saying that I had only given him the key to finding the swing that he already possessed when we first met.

> "Michelangelo went to a block of marble and took away all that wasn't David."
> —Fred Shoemaker from 'Extraordinary Golf'

Learning from adversity

> "Erroneous beliefs not only cause bad golf shots; they also create a whole lot of bad outcomes in other areas of our lives."

Illness Strikes

My life came to a sudden halt in 1977 when I was diagnosed with Hodgkins Disease, a cancer of the immune system. I had had flu after moving house over the New Year but the symptoms just lingered on and on for several months. It took until late May to get to the bottom of things when I was sent to a specialist in Southampton. Unbeknown to me, the whole family had been given advance warning as to what was the likely result of this consultation but, after several months of doubt as to what was happening to me, I was delighted when Professor Whitehouse examined me and then put a name on my malaise. At last my illness had both an identity and a form of treatment. Little did I know that this life-threatening disease could only be cured at that time by such a draconian regime of radiotherapy, itself a bit of a killer?

I had become more and more debilitated even to the extent where I could no longer play golf. I used to get home from work in the evening and sit down in front of the television to enjoy my dinner. After eating, I would say to Caroline that I would go to bed as I was exhausted, though actually I was so tired that it was only when the last programme had ended (yes, tv finished completely at about eleven pm in those days) that I could summon the strength to get out of my armchair and go up the stairs to bed.

I went through a series of tests and operations to establish what type of Hodgkins I had and to what extent it had developed. Some of these were a walk in the park but others were pretty unpleasant. What was surprising, especially for someone as squeamish as me, was my ability to take all this in my stride. I developed a technique of taking my mind out of my body when they were doing awful things to me such as a lumbar puncture and put it up in a high corner of the ceiling. From there I would look down and say to myself "Now, let's see what they're going to do to you today!"

After a couple of months the doctors were ready to start the radiotherapy, which consisted of four sessions per week for five weeks. The first few sessions were fine but then the effects started to accumulate and I began to feel dreadful. For several days I couldn't even sip water without it coming straight back at me. I lost all appetite and any thought of getting food down was out of the question. I have never been a heavy build and had been somewhere around one hundred and fifty pounds for a height of one eighty eight cms (six foot two) before being ill and around one hundred and twenty pounds when I started radiotherapy. I hate to think just how thin I had become by the time the treatment finished. Philip remembers that I weighed ninety pounds at the end of the treatment but I must have dodged that bit of information in an effort to keep such unhelpful statistics from penetrating my mind.

It was a thirty-minute journey to the hospital and it had become a bit of a nightmare process to go so long without being sick. Eventually, having put my foot down and refusing to go again, I had been cajoled and even forced to get into the car to go for the treatment. I distinctly remember looking at myself in the mirror one day and thinking that I looked pretty bad, wondering if I could really come through all this. I couldn't face any more. But then I got to the last few radiotherapy sessions and could see the end in sight, giving me an emotional lift. At last I arrived at the jackpot, the twentieth and last session. Oh, what a sense of relief. What bliss to not have that journey anymore!

Well, that's what I thought at the time but I must tell you that the worst was yet to come. No, I don't mean more discomfort. What followed was all about my mind and how it reacted to a faulty belief. As naive as it now seems to me, and after much thought as to why it all went so wrong, I now understand that I had been expecting, quite logically, to feel better once the treatment was completed. However, because it was having a cumulative effect, the opposite happened. I got worse. It was like a switch had been activated and, with a feeling of new hope dashed, I plummeted from euphoria to the depths of a deep depression. So black, in fact, that Caroline called the doctor one day in fear that I was suicidal. We had been out shopping and had bought some new electric plugs. Fitting them required cutting the wires and I was using a sharp penknife. I think she thought that I was going to slash my wrists. Of course, I wasn't going to do anything of the kind. Remember, I'm far too squeamish for such a bloody act!

On that particular day I just couldn't see past the present. Where our minds usually store images of the future there was nothing other than a black void. So, when the young doctor called he must have been faced with a daunting situation and a possible suicide candidate. I thought he was very brave when, after listening to me for a while, he simply asked me what I was going to do about it. I assured him that I wasn't going to do anything. I just wanted to feel happy again!

Over the next few months my mind started to clear and I realised that I was going to live. I can still remember standing in my kitchen one sunny morning drinking a strawberry milkshake and marvelling at how wonderful such a simple pleasure can be after weeks of my taste buds being obliterated by the bitterness of the radiotherapy.

With this realisation came a burst of enthusiasm, excitement and new ambition. I also decided that I was going to be happy, no matter what happened in the future. To this day, I still hold to this philosophy. It doesn't matter what else is going on in your life, just be happy. As the Dalai Lama says in "The Art of Happiness", you can't be happy all the time but you can develop an underlying state of happiness that allows you to face difficult situations more effectively and get back to being happy again more quickly.

It took many years to understand the negative effect that this misconception of my state of health had provoked. My expectations had not been met and disappointment had taken a strong and relentless hold on me.

Armed with these new levels of motivation, I soon applied for the job as the Club Pro and Golf Director at the two-year old Staverton Park Golf & Country Club in Northamptonshire. The club secretary had no golf knowledge so my first interview was with the outgoing pro and now world famous, David Leadbetter. I was duly appointed and I find it difficult to believe that, just six months after the end of my treatment, I had a new job in a different part of the country. Caroline ran a riding stable in the New Forest with her mother and enjoyed an idyllic lifestyle. My reborn ambition required us to move and she took some persuading, I can tell you. Eventually, she agreed but her heart was never really anywhere but in Hampshire and she moved back three years later. I followed a couple of years afterwards when I became the Club pro at Stoneham Golf Club in Southampton.

The Power Of Beliefs

Before moving on to relate my experiments at Stoneham, which eventually led to 'La Danse du Golf', I must pause to reflect on the added insight I have gained during the process of my present partner, Bee's, current illness. She was recently diagnosed with cancer and, having completed the chemotherapy, has today, as I write this part of the book, started the second part of her treatment, twenty five sessions of radiotherapy.

I now have a much clearer understanding of what a partner goes through and thus what Caroline must have gone through when I was ill. Undoubtedly, the person suffering the illness and subsequent treatment is at the pointed end of the situation but not to be forgotten is the feeling of helplessness that the partner has to cope with. I know that I didn't take this into account thirty years ago. It was as if all my energy was being directed selfishly and instinctively towards surviving. If I'm honest, I was feeling sorry for myself and couldn't take on board the emotions she must have been going through. I was also thirty years younger and less experienced in life.

Bee is doing well and the prognosis is very positive. She is coping better than I did. Maybe, in my own small way, I'm coping better than Caroline did as an onlooker but she was only twenty-one-years old when I had my problem. The role reversal has been educational to say the least.

103

This morning, the radiologist spent time preparing her for the side effects of the radiotherapy and I was interested to hear her say that the peak would actually come two weeks after the last treatment. If only they had known the importance of this little gem of information when I went through my radiotherapy my life would have changed out of all recognition, not only in terms of avoiding the depression, but also the negative effects of it which stayed with me for quite some time afterwards.

Golf coaches and teachers must take into account the beliefs and expectations that golfers bring with them to the lesson tee. If we don't take the time to find out what their beliefs are we will undoubtedly miss out on important and essential pieces of the jigsaw. The young Doctor's question, "What are you going to do about it?" also taught me the power of asking a question instead of making a statement.

Stoneham Experiment

I had started to build confidence in people's ability to move freely and still hit the ball. In fact, it became more and more evident that, generally, the more they moved the better they hit the ball. The more they moved the more they turned and the less they sliced and hooked. So, I decided to see just how far this notion of movement could be taken.

Every time I was coaching a new golfer, someone who had literally never hit a golf ball before, I would ask them to hit some shots with their eyes closed. Virtually everyone, whether young, old, male or female, sporty or not, managed to hit the ball. They were more surprised than I was. I then asked them, with eyes open of course, to try hitting a shot or, at least, making some contact with the ball with excessive leg and foot movement. I even went as far as to get them to swing their front leg over their back foot as they swung the club away from the ball and vice-versa when they swung through the ball (see Greg in photos 13 & 14). Admittedly, I didn't ask for a full shot just a half swing. Surprise, surprise, they could still hit the ball despite making most of the movement on one foot. Now, I asked them to do the same but with their eyes closed again. Well, surprise turned to astonishment, as the ball would often fly away with a lovely "click" as it was struck nicely off the middle of the club. I was so impressed that I started to try it out on just about everyone.

Photo 13   Photo 14

Golfers believe that they hit a bad shot because they move too much or lift their heads or take their eyes off the ball and here was proof of the very opposite. I still use this technique on a regular basis today because, sadly, I find that the majority of golfers still believe that they should keep their eyes fixed on the ball, their heads as still as possible and their feet glued to the ground on the back swing. With such little change in this area over the last twenty years, I think you can see why I feel the need to go public. If general standards are to improve in golf there must be a change in the way we view our basic human skills. Studies of the brain show that we only use a small percentage of its capabilities. Experiments have also found that the predetermined views of the teacher can radically influence the performance of the pupil.

A trial was carried out in which a group of students was split in two by random choice. The teachers of the first half were told that the students were of exceptional ability whereas the second group's teachers were told they were just average. The students in the first group went on to achieve great success and the second group achieved only average results. The teachers of the first group unknowingly displayed more confidence and enthusiasm for their students than the teachers of the second group. We coaches have a pivotal role in the education of our students and must guard against preconceived and judgemental attitudes. We must display more confidence in our students and not be frightened to attack the outdated misconceptions which form the basis of all the unsolicited advice that happens every day on every golf course everywhere in the world.

When we coach a new golfer who is finding it difficult to make good contact with the ball, it is easy to fall into the trap of thinking, "This person can't do it." Of course, if you believe this you will pass it on to your student without being aware that you're doing so. If you then encourage him or her to stay as still as possible, he or she will never gain confidence in movement and get locked into a system which says, "I'm not good enough to move like a good player so I'll just keep everything as 'controlled' as possible." Yes, I'm sure you can see the result: a static, stiff and awkward attempt to hit the ball with much more effort than is actually required and the development of debilitating self doubt and destructive negative self images.

Things turn out best for the people who make the best of the way things turn out."

—Art Linkletter – American Humanist, Journalist & TV Personality – born 1912

Quick Therapy

"The more quality questions I ask, and the less I talk, the more rapidly and effectively my clients learn!"

Coaching Raymond

I promised to tell you about Raymond and the 'quick therapist' story. Following on from my experience with the very stiff young lady whose golf was transformed by relaxing and dancing, and many other similar situations, my confidence had grown in the way I was coaching. Just as golfers gain confidence when they see and feel their shots being struck with more and more authority, so my confidence increased by what I was seeing and experiencing literally on a daily basis.

It was several years later when I was the General Manager at the wonderful Les Bordes club near Orleans that I met Raymond. There was no pro at the club at that time and, as well as managing the three golf courses and a forty-bedroom hotel, in my spare time (!) I filled the role of occasional coach. Raymond was staying at Les Bordes for his annual weeklong visit. His partner, Christiane, was a regular golfer but Raymond only had time to play once or twice a year. He loved Les Bordes so much that, despite the punitive nature of the course (Par 72, SSS 76, slope 149 and water on twelve holes), and the rather poor level of his game, he couldn't resist it. It is a most beautiful and relaxing place to be and he used it as a golfing retreat, well away from the busy and pressured world he usually lived in. He worked as a business coach and, at that time, was helping France Telecom's top management come to terms with privatisation.

When he hit his first few shots I found myself confronted by one of the worst swings I'd ever witnessed. Sorry, Raymond, but I can't be any more diplomatic than that. His posture was appalling; he had the strongest hooker's grip I'd ever seen and he had no idea about weight transference. He finished every shot on the back foot and found it virtually impossible to keep any kind of balance. To say that he was stiff, uncoordinated and awkward in everything he did would be an understatement. He seemed incapable of striking the ball with any sense of timing and, on the rare occasion the ball flew in the air, it was literally sprayed to all corners of the practice range, both to the right and the left.

I began by asking him what he would teach me if I was a friend he had brought to the practice range for the first time and who had never held a golf club before in his life. He duly told me that my eyes should be glued to a specific mark on the ball, my head should stay absolutely still, the club should go back on a straight line for as long as possible, my leading arm (my left arm as I am a right handed player) should be kept as straight as possible and I should keep my feet firmly on the ground until my right foot turned as I went through the ball. I should then extend both arms toward the target and keep my head down for as long as possible after the ball had gone. He finished by saying that if possible, I should look at the spot where the ball had been until the very end of the swing.

Having established that he was undoubtedly suffering the consequences of his own beliefs, and to be fair to him, he was indeed being totally faithful to them, I now knew that he needed to see the golf swing in a different light. But, of course, simply telling him that he was wrong was unlikely to be productive. Not only was he a coach himself, but he had also been a highly successful managing director. How does this type of person take to being told that he is wrong? I leave the response to your imagination.

As he had started by telling me the importance of looking at the ball, and to his surprise, I began by asking him to hit a shot with his eyes shut. At his first attempt the ball popped off the clubface with a nice click. Now he was even more surprised. I then asked him to hit a shot with his legs swinging, as Greg is doing in photos 13 & 14 on page 105. I think he thought I was mad but surprised himself some more when the ball again flew off the centre of the club and went about forty yards. The next, and possibly the most radical step, was to ask him to do the same again but with his eyes shut. Now he knew I was mad until the ball was struck cleanly and flew away about the same distance. When he opened his eyes to see the end of the ball's flight he looked back at me with a look of total disbelief on his face.

"How did you do that," I asked?

"Je ne sais pas! I don't believe what I just did," he said with more than a tinge of confusion in his voice.

"But you told me that you had to keep your feet on the ground, your eyes fixed on the ball, your arm straight and your head still. Let's see if I can help you to understand what has just happened."

We did 'La Danse du Golf' together and I asked him to find two aspects in this exercise that he would also find in a throwing movement. He replied with turning and weight shift. I then asked if he could feel any elements in 'La Danse du Golf' that he might find similar and useful in dancing. With a little help from me he duly came up with rhythm, balance, coordination and 'la souplesse.' At this point I asked him if he had, up to that point, found the golf swing to be easy, simple and natural. "Oh, no!" he replied with the type of expression on his face that amply reflected years of frustration and anguish. "Golf is difficult, technical, complex and unnatural."

"And how do you find 'La Danse du Golf,' I asked?

He was evidently finding it difficult to relate this to playing golf but answered cautiously.

"Yes, this feels quite easy," he said.

I could read the unspoken words in his mind, 'but what has this got to do with playing golf?'

I then asked him to make the same movement again but introducing, one by one, the instructions he would have given me as a total novice. He was a fairly heavily built man in his mid-forties and the tension and tightness of the new movement showed immediately on his face. "Mon Dieu!" he exclaimed, "qu'est-ce que c'est difficile! That's so difficult."

I suggested that he now try to hit some shots with the same feeling and movement that he had felt when doing 'La Danse du Golf' and he immediately looked like a different man. Before my very eyes he displayed superb rhythm and movement with excellent balance. He was hitting a four-iron off a low tee and, with his exaggerated hooker's grip I expected his new free movement to make the balls to go to the left and quite low. This can happen when the flow of your swing is suddenly liberated and you play with a closed clubface. Even I was surprised by the strike and flight of the balls as he hit a succession of beautifully struck, high, straight, long shots. The look on his face didn't need him to tell me that he had never hit the ball like this in his life before. He was astounded.

He suddenly turned to me and said, "Tu es un therapeute rapide." He was calling me a 'quick therapist.'

"What's that," I asked.

"It's what I do in my work as a business coach," he replied.

We ended up having dinner together that evening and he explained that his process was very similar to my way of coaching in that he asked a lot of questions in order to find out as much as possible about the people he was coaching and the way they thought. Armed with this information and knowledge he then knew exactly where he needed to work and how to formulate his input.

Raymond's ideas on 'quick therapy' are closely related to the Inner Game beliefs on awareness, themselves easily summarised by these words from Fritz Perls, founder of Gestalt Therapy, "Awareness cures, trying fails." All I had done for Raymond was to direct his awareness to certain points and given him options. He did the rest himself without in any way trying to change.

Quick Therapy In The Workplace

I was so impressed with his thoughts on coaching that I subsequently arranged for him to do a three-day seminar for my heads of department and their assistants. It proved to be a ground-breaking experience for those who took part. Raymond was a master of delivering a coaching session and I will always remember the positive way he operated. I was particularly touched by the story of his arrival as the new managing director in a company in the south of France some years earlier. After two days of receiving a constant stream of people coming into his office with complaints regarding what was wrong in the company he had had enough. His office was on the third floor and opposite the lift that most people had to take to get there. On the fourth day, when the lift door opened, a big notice on his office window met everyone. It read, *"Solutions – come straight in. Problems – go to the second door on the right and flush them down the toilet!"*

Possibly the most enlightening thing he did for me in my efforts to encourage everyone to work as a team was first to get us to score ourselves on the quality of our work in three different ways; individually, then in our departments, then as a whole team. Our results were collated and, later in the day, he displayed them for us all to see on a large screen. The maximum score was twenty and, before announcing our scores, he had told us that a team average score of zero to twelve represented a group of individuals working together, a score of thirteen to sixteen meant that the group worked together as a team, but that a score of seventeen or over represented a 'winning team.'

The average score we had given ourselves for the quality of our individual work was fourteen. The average for our departments was sixteen but the average for the whole workforce was only twelve. This translated into the fact that we saw ourselves as not bad individually but better in our small departmental teams. However, we saw ourselves as pretty poor when taken as a large group. In other words, I'm just OK, my team is pretty good, but the rest of you are rubbish! When faced with this feedback, all sitting together in the same room, there were looks of embarrassment on many faces.

This one realisation proved to be a watershed moment and the group went on to discover new ways of communicating with each other, an area which had been causing some major problems in the smooth running of the business. Merci, Raymond!

Raymond didn't need to say much to us or 'tell' us what to do because what he had done was given us thought provoking awareness and knowledge about the way we were and the way we interacted with each other. As the days and weeks went by the difference was as astounding as the change in his golf. I had known that we weren't working as a winning team but I knew instinctively that simply telling staff to communicate and work more as a team wasn't going to change anything. Funnily enough, it often produces more tension between people and causes a style of culture in which nobody thinks they're to blame.

> "Preconceived notions are the locks on the door to wisdom"
>
> —Merry Browne - Author

Part 2:
Increasing Your Confidence

The Worst Word In Golf

"Questions are powerful tools in any coaching situation. However, for golfers there is a one-word question that is powerfully negative. WHY?"

$$P = p - i$$

THE success of Positive Impact Golf coaching can be split into 2 distinct areas. Firstly, by removing the obstacles of false beliefs you will improve the way you swing the club. This leads to better ball striking, a better ball flight and a basic improvement in the quality of your golf shots. Feeling and seeing these results will boost your confidence and increase the pleasure you get from playing golf. Secondly, by understanding and modifying the way you react to bad shots you will reduce the amount of interference you have been unwittingly putting in your own way.

You will be liberated from self-imposed criticism and become more positive about yourself and your game.

Just take a few moments to reflect on this simple but profound equation, developed by Timothy Gallwey; **"Performance equals Potential minus Interference."** In the first 8 chapters you have read about the ways in which you can inhibit your natural ability to swing a golf club. These false beliefs, in themselves, interfere with the flow of natural, rhythmical movement. In the remaining chapters of the book I want to open your mind to other ways in which you may be adding to this interference.

We are all coaches in some area of our lives and we would do well to keep this equation at the forefront of our minds. At its best, coaching will 'shine the diamonds' in people. At worst, dictatorial and instruction based teaching can, in itself, become an additional interference to people's potential to perform the task they are learning!

Turning Bad Shots Into Opportunities To Learn

How you react to your bad shots is one of the most essential aspects to both improving your game and, most importantly, enjoying your golf to the full. When I watch many players they give the impression of hating the game rather than loving it. Their reactions go from anger, to frustration, to disbelief – "Oh, no! I've never played so badly in my life" – and even to throwing the club away in disgust. The simple answer to Q9 ('what should you do after a bad shot?') is to do and say NOTHING. Every bad shot is an opportunity NOT TO REACT. Reacting is just another bad habit that can be easily changed.

Let me give you a quote from the first page of the first chapter in Ernest Jones' 1937 book "Swing The Club Head".......

"I want to point out wherein I feel most people make mistakes. Briefly summed up, I think the fundamental difficulty lies in a negative instead of a positive approach; golfers start from a premise of trying to find out what is wrong when the shot does not come off satisfactorily, instead of getting back to the positive consideration of what it is that causes the shot to prove satisfactory. That this approach is a natural result of the system of teaching employed by their instructors is all the more unfortunate."

I believe that nothing has changed since Ernest wrote this over 70 years ago. If anything, we have increased this negative tendency with all the modern technology at our disposal and the ability it gives us to analyse our swing in every detail.

Less Is More

One day I was at a driving range helping my brother-in-law with his game and there was a young woman in the bay next to us with a friend who evidently knew more about the game than she did. She had obviously not been playing for long but had the beginnings of quite a nice swing. She hit one or two good shots and then topped one. "Why did I do that," she asked? Her friend explained what had happened in some detail. She hit a few reasonable shots and then one that went out to the right. "Why did it go to the right," she asked? Again, he told her why. A few shots later and she hit one low to the left. Yes, you've guessed it; she asked the same question again and was rewarded by another onslaught of data and information. This pattern continued over a period of about 20 minutes and her swing got worse and worse until she eventually became very frustrated as her shots were all going awry and the good early shots had totally disappeared. So, too, did her nice swing. You could just see the effect of all this confusing advice as she fought to control all the elements she had been encouraged to think about.

This typical situation happens every day anywhere and everywhere golf is played. Her friend was at fault for giving her an overload of information whilst she was at fault for asking for it! Of course both parties meant well. She just wanted to learn and improve and he just wanted to help. The thoughtful and experienced golf coach would never have fallen into this trap. If you are a young golf coach, please heed my plea and take great care to judge how much advice your student can take at any time. Not only must you be careful to give the right amount of digestible advice in a given session, but you must also give your student enough time to absorb and integrate your advice before moving on to the next step. Going too fast may well cause you to lose your student's confidence through excessive advice or, at least, cause a slowing down of the learning process.

In 2005 I passed a diploma course in Performance Coaching, a workplace-based coaching course not related to golf or sport. One of the major aspects it confirmed to me was that I had been right to be conscious of overloading students with too much advice in any given period. It is the student's ability to digest and assimilate information that sets the speed and agenda of learning and not the coach or any pre-determined regime. Only in group coaching for beginners can you stick to a pre-formulated programme to some extent and even then it is only effective for a short period before each individual requires tailored attention.

By all accounts, Harvey Pennick would never let close friends Ben Crenshaw and Tom Kite be present at a lesson he was giving to the other one of them. He understood the potential damage of listening to the content of someone else's lesson. We've all done it. A snippet of advice sounds so good and we are immediately enticed to leave our own thought process to one side for the lure of finding the secret of golf in someone else's learning process.

The 'Why' Syndrome

In his wonderful 1887 book entitled 'The Art of Golf,' Sir Walter Simpson wrote that there was, in his opinion, a major difference between the 'professional' and the 'amateur' golfer. The term professional was his way of differentiating between the good players of the time and those less talented who he called the amateurs. In those days, the professional golfer had come through the ranks of being a caddy and was generally an uneducated man. Amateur golfers were mainly wealthy and well educated people. He believed that the 'professionals' knew that they had heeled, topped, sclaffed or toed their shots but didn't have the intelligence to analyse why it had happened. Let me quote you his words from so long ago......

"Still, the amateur golfer must be allowed to theorise to some extent. It is a necessary concession to him as a thinking animal. Within indicated limits, it will do no harm... It is noticeable that the amateur (in distinction from the professional) asks, 'Why did I heel – top – sclaff – toe?' – and, if golf is to be a pleasure not a business, he must be allowed to ask these things. If not, he is apt to give up the game as too simple. On the other hand, if he does not recognise 'hitting the ball' as his business, and theory as his recreation, he becomes so bad a player that he nearly gives up."

Asking 'Why?' is dangerous for two reasons. Firstly, it allows your golfing partners to give you another dose of unwanted and potentially damaging advice and, secondly, it sets your own mind to thinking about what might have gone wrong on the last shot.

Let me expand on my thoughts about the amount and effect of unsolicited advice in golf. I believe it to be the major factor in limiting the average players' progress in the game, so much so that I would call it a disease.

Over the course of a couple of games plus the odd session at the driving range you may well be given half a dozen explanations and tips about the way you play by seemingly kind people. Add to this the ones that your own imagination is throwing at you and you begin to see the growing complexity of the situation. Which of these gems of advice is correct? Of course, you don't know! But, just in case they're right you're going to keep them in your mind anyway. Don't forget what I told you earlier; ninety five per cent of our actions are controlled by the subconscious mind so you are cramming all these ideas into the 5 per cent that you think you have under your own control. When you get out onto the course you have a juggling match with them all, whilst your subconscious has its own agenda and is doing its own thing. Is it little wonder that most golfers find the game so complicated? It's just like those guys you see on stage with all the spinning plates. As soon as they're all spinning one starts to wobble. In golf, we rarely get all our plates spinning fully at the same time.

Web Of Confusion

Let me tell you about Ken who came to me as a frustrated 59 year old, 12-handicap golfer. His life's ambition was to get into single figures. After a while it became apparent to me that he had good natural ability but was suffering from over-analysis of his swing. Together we discovered what he now describes as a kind of spider's web of technical detail that was blocking his talent. He used to come up to the driving range and work on his technique, eventually finding something that got him hitting the ball well.

"Ah!" he would say to himself, "I've got it!"

He would go home happy and come back the next time to confidently use the same formula only to find that it didn't work anymore. He would search and search until he hit on something else then go and play a few holes, trying it out on the course. After only a couple of holes he would find that the new swing formula wasn't performing so return to the driving range to work out what had gone wrong. Of course, the more he repeated this process the more confused he became and the more strands got added to the spider's web. When we met, his natural talent was hidden behind the many layers that he had unwittingly added over the years. His commendable efforts to improve had complicated his mind and blocked him from using his latent ability. He was so busy asking himself "WHY" that he had become incapable of playing naturally.

When I asked Ken to hit balls with no thought at all, he was more than dubious about my intentions. However, when he found that he could hit it well with his eyes shut and no thought of how he was doing it he began to see the light that had been hidden by the web. Twelve months later and not only had he achieved his ambition of getting down to nine but was playing consistently to it and was even confident that he could reduce it again. He has since come down to eight. To say that he really enjoys his golf these days is an understatement. If you see him one day, please don't tell him that I told you that he still sometimes looks a bit bemused by the fact that he has progressed so well by letting go of the spider's web and thinking less!

Ken's story is not an unusual one and many of you will relate to it. If only I had been given the same advice when I first rejected my natural, unthinking swing for the world of mechanics and technique who knows where I may have ended up? I could have so easily at that early time taken away the few layers of marble and found my golfing David as per Fred Shoemaker's quote rather than adding a multitude of new layers over the ensuing years.

Be Positive

When you hit a bad shot, either on the course or when practising, here is a simple habit to develop. If you know or sense immediately what you've done wrong that's great. Don't, however, fall into the trap of trying to avoid making the same error on the next shot but convert the information into a positive statement of intent on the next shot.

For example, you know you just lost your balance at the end of the previous swing so will be tempted to say "don't lose your balance this time." The human brain doesn't register negatives like the word 'don't.' When told 'don't think of a blue cow,' all we can see in our minds is a blue cow. So, a more effective way of talking to yourself is "come on, let's see you get to a nice balanced finish. You know you hit it better when you do." Talk to yourself as you would talk encouragingly to a child. We all have a 'child within' who really detests being incessantly told that what he or she is doing is wrong.

When you hit a bad shot and you just don't know what you've done then simply put a cross against it and carry on to the next shot with no analysis. It's enough to recognise that it was bad and to feel that it wasn't the same as the sensation you get on a successful shot. This should fuel you with the positive intention of using your powers of feel to find the good swing again and, with a bit of practice, you can learn to trust yourself to get you back to experiencing the good shots again straight away.

You can always use something to trigger you back into a confident and relaxed state thus counteracting the gain of negative energy from your bad shots. 'La Danse du Golf' is an excellent way of re-sourcing yourself in the simplicity of good movement. Another way is to hold the butt end of the club lightly between thumb and forefinger at about the height of your stomach. Let it swing from side to side, back and forth like a pendulum, feeling the weight of the club head. Once it has done this a couple of times just pick up the movement yourself, coordinating your weight shift with the motion in the club head, especially in your foot action. Within seconds you will relax and feel better rhythm flood back into your body. You can feel more with your feet than you imagine including several of our big six basics; weight transfer, rhythm, balance and coordination. You can even feel whether you are turning as you should be doing or moving laterally which provokes a swaying, sideways movement rather than the turning shift you are looking for.

Any other methods or non-technical tricks that you can employ to get you back to normal are valid and should never be discounted. By far the best training aid is called the Original SwingRite. It is a sort of swing simulator that looks like a shortened club without a head and it clicks as you swing it through the air despite the fact that there is no ball. The click sounds and feels like hitting a shot. What it does so effectively is to tell you how to swing a golf club without having to think about anything other than swinging. Golfers consistently swing it with better rhythm and motion than when they are hitting real shots. It's as if all the interferences disappear. There is no ball, no target and no result to take your attention away from the simple art of swinging the club. The more you practice with it the more you are encouraged to use the same improved swing when hitting shots. You would be advised to get one and use it regularly. Practice makes permanent so why not practice using your best swing until it becomes a habit rather than hitting balls with the same old swing faults? It was designed by Mindy Blake, a member at Wentworth, nearly fifty years ago and has truly passed the test of time.

I remember watching Gary Player, again at Wentworth, in what was then the Piccadilly World Match Play Championship. He hit a poor shot on one hole and then walked off only to stop a few yards later to rehearse the swing he felt he should have made. There was no analysis of the bad swing just enormous positive intent to make a good swing the next time and hit a good shot.

Let me end this chapter by repeating Ernest Jones' most instructive words:

"I want to point out wherein I feel most people make mistakes. Briefly summed up, I think the fundamental difficulty lies in a negative rather than a positive approach; golfers start from a premise of trying to find out what is wrong when the shot does not come off satisfactorily, instead of getting back to the positive consideration of what it is that causes the shot to prove satisfactory. That this approach is a natural result of the system of teaching employed by their instructors is all the more unfortunate"

—Ernest Jones – "Swing The Club Head" (1937)

The Way We Talk To Ourselves

"The words we use, and the language of the internal conversations we have with ourselves, are powerful tools which golfers should take great care in choosing."

The Two Selves Of The Inner Game

I was playing a Captain and Pro match at Staverton Park one Sunday morning. One of our opponents was a twenty four handicapper called Mike. This was in the days of twenty four being the maximum handicap available to men. I had to give him eighteen shots, one a hole. The first hole in those days was a long par four and he hit a lovely drive followed by a nice fairway wood to within thirty yards of the green. He proceeded to top his next shot about the same distance over the green to which he reacted by exclaiming, in a very frustrated tone, "Oh! So it's going to be one of those days!" My mind went from being anxious about the result to being confident that his prediction might well prove to be true. Indeed it was and we won easily.

In the very first chapter I promised to talk more about our internal conversations so let me tell you about the major influence Timothy Gallwey's Inner Game philosophy has had on my work as a golf coach. I read his first book, The Inner Game of Tennis, over twenty five years ago and learnt about his views on a different way of learning. Gallwey had withdrawn from mainstream higher education in the States when he became disillusioned by the institutionalised way in which teaching was developing. He felt that teaching had become 'teacher-centred' and that this approach inhibited the learning process. He began to coach tennis and was struck by how much his students talked to themselves on the court. He was intrigued by this dialogue and asked them who they were talking to. In most cases they said, "I'm talking to myself."

The essential part of the Inner Game coaching philosophy is Tim's discovery of the two selves, 'I' and 'myself,' which he calls Self One and Self Two. This represents the internal conversation we have with ourselves, especially when things go wrong. Self One is the conscious, analytical part of our mind whereas Self Two is the unconscious and naturally talented part of us. In short, Self One is often a destructive and negative influence. He's the little guy who sits on your shoulder telling you to be careful of all that can go wrong on the golf course. He tells you that you're no good and that it would have been better to stay at home and done the gardening. He's the guy who, if he was a caddy, you'd sack after only a few holes just to get him off your back!

When things are going well he doesn't say much but when things start to go wrong, or you are under pressure, he becomes over-active. He asks 'why' did you hit such a bad shot?' and then goes on to tell you to keep an eye on your grip, posture, alignment, rhythm, swing plane, etc., etc.

On the other hand, Self Two is the quiet, unobtrusive but highly capable guy who knows what to do and how to do it - if only Self One would recognise it and let him get on with doing things in a natural way. Unfortunately, Self One is a control freak so doesn't like to let go. He'll tell you what to do and how to do it and then heap criticism on you when you get it wrong. For example, you're playing a tee shot to a narrow fairway with bunkers all down the right hand side. "Don't go into the bunkers on the right," Self One commands, unwittingly and unwisely planting those bunkers firmly in your mind. Of course, he is the first one to treat you as an idiot when your ball sails unnervingly straight into one of those waiting traps, saying "But, I told you not to go near those bunkers!" He sometimes thinks that Self Two is deaf, blind and stupid.

Let me quote Tim again from his original book which, although it was written about tennis, could so easily be attributed to golf;

"The truth is, of course, that Self Two, which includes the unconscious mind and nervous system, hears everything, never forgets anything, and is anything but stupid. After hitting the ball firmly once, he knows forever which muscles to contract to do it again. That's his nature."

Wise coaches recognise this damaging, self-inflicted tendency in most golfers and can achieve remarkable results simply by helping their students to become aware of it. When you start to recognise the Self One voice for what it is and let Self Two have more say in what you do you will be amazed at the difference it makes.

I recently read an article by Dr Karl Morris in which he wrote that we humans are the only animals on the planet who think about the past and the future. All other animals, he stated, only react to the present situation. I agree with his analysis and would add that we are the only animals who have this internal conversation between Self One and Self Two. Can you imagine your dog saying to himself "You stupid fool, you keep chasing the neighbour's cat and you're never going to catch it? You're just too old and slow. I don't know why you bother. You'd do better to stay indoors and chew your bone"

Tim uses golf and tennis as coaching tools in all kinds of learning situations including business and work as he says that *the way you do something is the way you do anything.*' Understanding and improving the way you talk to yourself is, I believe, fundamental to increasing your enjoyment of the game of golf and can have a major impact in other areas of your life. Start listening to yourself as if the voice you can hear is someone else's and the subsequent awareness will allow you to free yourself from this previously unknown burden.

The simple truth is that we have a tendency to fall into negative 'self talk' in any area of our lives and possibly nowhere more than on the golf course. Become more aware of the words your Self One is using and take the pressure off yourself by quietening the 'bad caddy' in your head and start to encourage your Self Two to apply its talents to the situation.

Just as Donald Sutherland said in the movie 'Kelly's Heroes' when faced with someone who didn't have confidence in the plot to rob a bank behind enemy lines and kept interrupting with all the ways it could go wrong, "Hey, man, don't give me any more of those negative waves!" Not that I'm suggesting for a minute that you should carry out such a nefarious deed. I am just asking you to plug into the positives which exist all around you and, especially, in your own mind.

Adopting A Positive Attitude To Bad Shots

Just take a moment and read again the quote from Ernest Jones at the end of the previous chapter. I had always heard of him but had never read any of his writing. I had subconsciously dismissed him because he was from a bygone era and I saw myself as being very modern and forward thinking. I had, however, always felt an empathy with the title of his book, 'Swing The Club Head.' When I returned to daily coaching in 2006, after ten years of managing golf clubs, I had a thirst for knowledge and decided that I would read everything I could get my hands on. I got hold of his book a few months after having decided on the name 'Positive Impact Golf.' I'll tell you more later about how and why I chose this title but you can imagine my amazement when I read that passage that Jones wrote at the beginning of his book.

It was as if he was talking to me, telling me that I was absolutely right to spend so much time on this aspect of the game. 'Positive Impact Golf,' seeks to demystify the golf swing and translate it into terms that the average golfer can understand. Our coaches soon find out why and where golfers are being held back. When released from erroneous concepts players find that improvement comes rapidly. But the other area that helps golfers to actually improve on the golf course is their attitude to bad shots and how they flourish and enjoy their game more when they opt out of the self-critical and debilitating "WHY?" syndrome. After all is said and done, when was the last time you played a round of golf without hitting a bad shot? Indeed, when was the last recorded round of golf played at any level that didn't include a bad shot? When did even Tiger Woods last play a round of golf without hitting a bad shot? Do you stand on the first tee imagining a fault free round? If you do, my friend, you are in for a torrid time?

Golf is an inherently inconsistent game. Inconsistency is part of its very makeup and its very infrastructure. You can't get away from it. In the game of golf there is one certain and CONSISTENT fact. Golf is the most INCONSISTENT game in the world!

You can, however, reduce the inconsistencies to an acceptable level by adopting a more reasonable attitude to your bad shots. If there's nothing good to say after a particular shot, say NOTHING and do NOTHING! Just put your club in the bag and walk forward to the next shot keeping yourself in the best possible state of mind to hit the next one. Once you get angry, frustrated and disappointed, you will heap tension on your game and come off the golf course deflated, dejected and exhausted. Remember what tension does? It steals your feel and robs you of your talent.

I sometimes do a 'tongue-in-cheek' demonstration to show how easy it is to develop the right attitude to bad shots. I ask my student to agree that it is a nice day to be here playing golf. I hit a good shot and repeat that it is a nice day, especially now that I've hit it well and the ball has sailed away into the distance. I then hit a rank bad shot followed by the question "Is it still a nice day?" Of course, nothing has changed unless I let the bad shot change my attitude and state of mind. Note my use of the words 'unless I let.' Yes, it's my choice to let it affect me; the bad shot can't do anything on its own.

From Good To Great

As you may well know, Bobby Jones was a remarkable golfer. He first qualified for the US Amateur Championship at the age of fourteen and won a couple of matches. Although he became a very good player he never seemed to fulfil that early promise. He was, in fact, a fiery character who set himself such a high standard that he got very upset with anything less than perfection. He was once threatened with a ban from competitive golf when he threw a club that hit a lady spectator. He reviewed his golf and decided that he needed to make some changes, subsequently deciding on three essential points:

1. I must be prepared for the making of mistakes
2. I must choose the strategy for every shot to give myself the widest possible margin of error
3. I must accept having to do some scrambling and not be disappointed if the amount of it is more than normal

He went on to win the Grand Slam at the age of 28 in 1930 before retiring immediately due to increasing health problems. His success came from his change of attitude not from any modification to his swing technique.

> "Profound understanding requires attention to what lies behind the visible surface"
>
> —W. Timothy Gallwey –from The Inner Game of Work

135

Course Management

"Successful people know how to manage themselves and how to get the best out of other people in their business affairs. However, they rarely seem to take these abilities to the golf course."

Pete The Butcher

I'VE told you about how my own game lost its way by applying a technical 'method' that I now believe to be flawed for most people. I have given you my views on the six basics of 'La Danse du Golf,' turning, weight shift, rhythm, balance, coordination and 'souplesse.' I have talked to you about certain other misconceptions and how these beliefs can block your natural ability to do something as simple as swinging a golf club and hitting a little white ball. I have told you about the importance of movement and the dangers of tension.

I have gone on to tell you about the negative way we tend to talk to ourselves and how that dictates our reaction to bad shots. I now want to tell you a bit about course management, or more precisely, how to manage yourself on the course.

When I met Pete he was a complete beginner who came on Staverton Park's winter golf trip to Majorca in 1980. Pete is a very successful butcher who now supplies the majority of the country's Michelin star chefs with top quality meat products. He had bravely accepted to make up the numbers on our trip at the last minute when someone dropped out. He had hardly played on a course before and threw himself in at the deep end. We are still very good friends to this day and I have come to understand that this decision was far from uncharacteristic. He is a particularly competitive person in sport and in business and he just loves a challenge.

One day, a few months after returning from the trip, I was waiting for him to arrive at Staverton for a playing lesson. I had finished my previous session and was waiting for him on the practice range just by the first tee. No surprise, he was late, eventually appearing at speed, running from the clubhouse. Having apologised for being late and adding that he needed to be back in his office for an appointment in just over a couple of hours, we didn't have time to prepare with a few shots on the range as we know you should so went straight onto the tee. He hit his drive along the ground off the heel of the club and the ball settled fifty yards away in the long rough to the left of the teeing area.

When we got to his ball he reached for his fairway wood. I asked him what he was intending to do with his second shot and he explained that he needed to make up for such a poor drive and get the ball as far up the fairway as possible. Pete is possibly the most positive character I've ever met and I sensed he wouldn't like my advice but I knew that we were both in for a bad experience if he hit another poor shot. His internal clock was already ticking at high speed after a fast drive from work and, in an effort to rush round the nine holes he was likely to get even more stressed and uptight as the holes passed.

"Pete, your chances of hitting a clean shot from that lie are slim for three reasons. You have already hit a bad drive, you are in a bit of a state due to arriving late and you're choosing a straight-faced club from a bad lie.

Let's imagine various outcomes. You get lucky and hit a good shot but there is a bunker on the corner of the dog-leg just at the distance you normally hit your five-wood. Not a sensible play. A more likely result is that you hit a bad shot and feel lousy as you walk up to your third shot. A few holes later, and after more bad shots, you are beginning to tell yourself that you should have stayed in the office. Why don't you use the same skills you demonstrate in your everyday business life by not making two mistakes in a row? Hit a nice, easy seven-iron. You're more likely to succeed and will feel a lot better about yourself. You also won't reach the bunker but will leave a relatively easy third shot to the green."

"But I can get it out with the 5-wood and there's a bit of room to get past that bunker on the left," responded Pete with a look of fighting determination etched on his face.

"Pete, every golfer thinks like that. It's exactly why most golfers don't play regularly to their handicaps. Of course you can do it, but how many times would you succeed out of ten attempts?"

I have since learnt that one of Pete's philosophies in life is that you should do the opposite of what everyone else is doing. When the market is down we all sell our shares because we lose confidence. The clever investor buys when we're selling and sells when we're buying. We lose money because we respond to the market and are easily influenced by what the masses are doing rather than predicting and precipitating the trends ourselves.

My last comment struck a chord and it was if a little light lit up in his head. He hit a lovely seven-iron well short of the bunker and walked up the fairway like a man free from the worries and anxieties he had displayed a few minutes earlier. As luck would have it, and maybe we make our own luck, he hit a nice shot onto the green and holed the putt for a par!

As we played the remaining holes I went on to explain in more detail how most golfers rarely play to their handicaps and I distinctly recall telling him that anyone who does so will win far more than his fair share of competitions and matches. Pete seemed to grasp the point that I was making in that the handicapping system in the UK doesn't produce a handicap based on the average score but is purely the result of a player's best two or three rounds of the year. I have since done studies of competition scores and have proved that the average score is quite a few shots above the average handicap of those competing.

It's a simple fact that in any competition nearly all competitors play above their handicap and only a few either play to it or below. We play most of our golf over our handicap and so often go home disappointed. The next time you go to your club look at the results from recent competitions and you'll see exactly what I mean.

Pete, despite a butchers swing (sorry Pete!), has become one of the most consistent players to his handicap that I know. He has learnt to optimise his talents and uses great course management. The way he manages himself through eighteen holes is testament to the significant philosophy he learnt that day at Staverton.

I can't leave this section on Pete without talking about his attitude to learning and change. From the first moment I started to help him he was comfortable with the idea of change. Far too many people wish to improve but have some sort of instinctive barrier to change. It's as if they're saying to the coach, "Please, make me better but don't change anything!" It's often said that kids learn more quickly because they don't fear change as much as adults. I don't buy the opinion that adults can't change quickly. It's all a question of attitude.

I know Pete believes that the world is always changing and if you don't change you'll end up out of step with the natural world around you. His attitude to change is, in a sense, out of step with many people's reticence to change and allows him to fulfil his potential on the golf course and is a major factor in his success in business. In changing so readily he immediately puts himself in the opposite lane compared to most people.

Embracing Change

Why don't you try turning up for your next golf lesson with the idea that you are looking forward to changing something? Not only will you make life easier for your coach, but you'll also learn more quickly. If you're a coach, why not work at your ability to promote and develop your client's ability to change? You must already know the power of positively and wholeheartedly believing in the golfer's latent ability. After all is said and done, you are the catalyst to helping the player plug into this ability. I often remind the coaches who work with me and the coaches I coach that the client comes to us with the problem but he or she also has the solution.

So many coaches and teachers think that it is up to them to find all the faults, analyse them and provide all the solutions.

141

Fred Shoemaker calls the tendency to search continuously for quick fixes the 'culture of golfers.' In other words, there is something wrong so I must find out what it is and fix it. He goes to great length in his books 'Extraordinary Golf & 'Extraordinary Putting' to tell us that this is not only futile but also increases confusion in our games.

I remember the words of Jean-Claude, my doctor in France, who said to me one day, "What I like about the way you coach is that you give me the feeling that you're only helping me to find something that I already knew."

Coaching presented in this way doesn't confront the golfer's fear of change as much as traditional methods do. The over technical approach, with its constant desire to get you in different and unnatural positions, is fraught with difficulty and strongly suggests that, in order to bene-fit from your lessons, you need to accept a period of hard work during which you will be required to hit hundreds of balls on the practice range and possibly get worse before you get better. For the average golfer this is not always desirable nor is it practical.

There are occasions when a technical fault requires attention and, when that time is right, you may have to face up to the fact that you need to work at it for a while, but, preferably, I avoid this style of coaching. I have also spent many years looking for and adopting sym-pathetic ways in which the more technical aspects of golf can be easily integrated by golfers.

"But these guys play by mechanical means with positions. I don't see how they can ever play doing that. I have always felt you have to play golf by feel. All athletes, when they get in pressure situations, revert to what they know. I don't think you are going to revert to mechanics. I think you revert to feel."

—Jack Nicklaus – Winner of 18 Majors

Managing Your State

"We often play badly because we are not in the right STATE to play our best golf. Knowing how to control your state rather than being controlled by it is not as complicated as it may seem."

Identifying The Real Problem

I don't know how many times I must have gone through the following scenario when coaching? The golfer in front of me was playing well the last time we met but today it's just not happening. I know the player's swing and, in truth, it doesn't look much different from the last time. I'm not saying much because I'm taking time to look, study, analyse and get some feedback by asking some questions. Let me give you a recent example of how outside influences can interfere with your performance.

Mick had been improving steadily since we met a couple of years ago but a recent session was marred by an unusually high number of bad shots. He is a five-handicapper who is normally quite consistent.

My mind was trained in the early years to look for the technical solution and I have to admit that part of me still wanted to do this, no doubt my Self One. Luckily for my clients I have long ago learnt to control this tendency and so took more time to find out where the real problem lay. He was obviously not swinging the club or hitting the ball as well as usual but I soon found the nub of the problem when I asked how things were off the golf course. He began by saying that things were fine but added in a throw away sort of manner that he hadn't had much space for himself recently. "Why's that," I asked. "Oh! I've been up and down the motorway all week and everyone seems to have wanted a bit of me."

Well, look no further. The fact is that he was so wound up that he wasn't even waiting for the ball to land before he had another one in place for the next shot. His internal clock had been accelerating all week and he was far from relaxed. It took no more than a few shots hit with plenty of time in between to calm him down. I suggested that he slow down his actions, breath more freely and deeply and this allowed him to slow his inner clock. Add to this the realisation of what was the true cause of his problems and he started hitting the ball as normal within minutes. He got rid of the bad state and got himself back into the right state with no difficulty at all.

Please note that I hadn't told him that he was swinging the club too quickly and I hadn't told him to slow down, both futile bits of advice.

Those of you of a certain age will remember the 1981 Open Championship at Royal St. George's when Jack Nicklaus uncharacteristically shot a first round score of eighty three. Just before teeing off he had been told that one of his sons had been involved in a car accident in USA. He was evidently in a state of shock wherein his concentration on golf was shattered. When he got off the course he was informed that it was only a minor incident and he was able to talk to his unhurt son on the telephone. He improved by seventeen shots on day two shooting a sixty-six!

Sometimes things go wrong and we immediately focus on our technique. Be careful not to question your swing when, in reality, your current problem may have nothing to do with that at all.

John And Andy

In his excellent book, 'Quantum Golf,' Kjell Enhager tells the story of John Smith, a highly successful American businessman who plays off eighteen and who has got to that point that many golfers get to at some stage when he decides to give the game up. So disappointed and embarrassed has he become with his game that he just can't stand it anymore. Hands up if you've never felt those same emotions!

A last straw of hope is offered to this poor man when the Club Pro gives him details of an old guru coach and John grasps it and duly flies across the States to see if this Linc St. Clair fella' can unlock the great golfer within. You see, like everyone who plays this game, John knows that he should be better. After all, over the years, he has struck some marvellous shots and played many brilliant holes. OK, he's rarely put them all together in the same round and certainly never been able to sustain a run of form for longer than a couple of weeks, but he just feels that he should be able to perform to a better standard. In the world of work he is a consistent 'high performer' who rarely experiences failure and finds it difficult to accept the bad shots on the golf course.

I won't ruin the reading of Quantum Golf for you but Linc starts by asking what John does well and which club is his favourite. After protesting that he does nothing well, Linc quietly insists until John replies, "Ok, I don't know why, but I can do anything I want with a three-wood." Linc asked John to show him some three-wood shots. He hit a succession of lovely shots. Linc simply asks John to approach all clubs with the same confidence that he has with his three-wood.

Just recently, I have been helping Andy with his game. He is also a very successful entrepreneur and businessman who came to me in desperation as a sixteen handicapper who was getting to the same point as John of giving the game up because playing golf had ceased to be a pleasure. In fact, it had become a true nightmare and Andy couldn't see any point in putting himself through the trauma of playing badly, especially in front of his golfing friends who are never shy about ribbing him, or anyone else for that matter, after a calamitous shot. His problem was woods off the tee and, in particular, a three-wood off the first tee.

Let's imagine the inner state of these two golfers, John and Andy, with a three-wood in their hands. John is relaxed and comfortable as he expects to hit a good shot. Sometimes, it doesn't come off but he takes it philosophically and carries on in the knowledge that it was just a blip and the next one will be fine. On the other hand, Andy feels tense as his mind throws up all sorts of bad shots including tops, hooks and slices. When he hits a rare good one he treats it as an accident and carries on knowing that the next one will most likely be awful. His quota of good three-woods for the round has just been spent.

With a five-iron in their hands the roles are completely reversed. John feels like he has a foreign object in his hands that tighten in an effort to gain some semblance of control. The tension creeps from his hands to his arms and up into his shoulders like an invading enemy and his swing starts as if he is in a race to get the thing done before the invader gets to his very soul. As I am sure you can imagine, John's rhythm and balance are totally compromised and the resulting poor shot is no surprise as he hardly gets through to any kind of finish. What happened to that smooth, fluid swing with the three-wood?

How is Andy getting on? Surprise, surprise, his tension levels have reduced as soon as he got the club out of the bag. The invading enemy, so present on his tee shot, seems to have packed its bags and headed for some other defenceless golfer on an adjacent fairway, probably John. His muscles relax and he produces a rhythmical, smooth swing and finishes the shot in a composed and balanced position as the ball flies towards its target.

Nothing is truer than the old proverb about one man's meat being another man's poison but, in golfing terms, we don't need to accept it. With a little bit of mind gymnastics we can persuade ourselves to do anything.

One day I was with Jim, a solicitor and member at Barton-on-Sea. He had taken a few lessons over the previous six months and his game was progressing well. He told me that everything was working well even his four-iron, but the three-iron was still giving him a hard time and could we have a look at it. I asked him to hit a few mid-irons to warm up and, sure enough, he was swinging well and hitting the ball really nicely. "Ok," I said, "just before trying your three-iron let's see a couple of those good shots with your four-iron." I surreptitiously handed him the three-iron without saying a word and, lo and behold, he hit two beautiful shots. When I asked him to look at which club he had been hitting his face broke out into a wide and knowing smile. "Yes, sir, you've been had," I admitted, "but only in a positive and encouraging way, I hope."

Your Personal Notebook

Now, as promised, let me respond to Question 10 and talk about what you should do after a round of golf. You will have invariably hit some good and some bad shots. You will often come off the course with the sentiment that you could have played better golf. It happens to you and it happens regularly to every golfer I've ever met. So, how do we still manage to gain something positive from the experience?

Starting your 'Three Best Shots Book' and making sure that you commit to writing it up after every round will, in itself, be an important and practical step in the right direction. Even on those days when you think that there was nothing good to put down you'll be surprised to discover, for example, that you did hole a twenty-five-footer on the last green or did nearly hole your approach to the third or started with a glorious drive off the first tee in front of a crowd. The truth is that, just in the same way it is impossible to play eighteen holes with nothing but perfect shots, so is it impossible to play without the odd good, even perfect shot.

This technique will allow you to register and highlight the good things you do whilst letting go of the bad things, and it only takes a few minutes to do. Over a period of time you will fill your memory banks with successes and we all know that success breeds success. Probably the biggest challenge facing golfers is that of finding enough positives in the way they play to be able to achieve this. Reading back through your notebook will help you to recall those good shots and, most poignantly, to remember the feeling you had when you played them. When you have been doing this for a few months you will find that you have recorded good shots in all departments of the game, which in itself, is a powerful realisation.

Of course it will also highlight areas that do not appear, thus helping you to identify parts of your game that may need a little more attention. It will surely help your coach to be more effective in helping you to progress, as your feedback will be based on fact rather than emotion. It will help you to tell your coach how you're doing over a period of time rather than just how you played last time.

You might also think to record your lesson notes in this book, so that it becomes something that has never been published before, i.e. a golf book written by you about your game. Every writer of a golf book hopes to speak to the reader in a personal manner. I hope to have achieved that myself. But, noting the parts of this and other books you read in your own notebook will help you to remember issues and points that are pertinent to your game and put those little nuggets of advice into practice. Of course, be aware of any overload in this domain so as not to fall into the same trap as Ken.

You will recall that I asked you to score yourself from zero to ten in certain areas of your game. This, in my experience, is a far better way of sensing how you are progressing as opposed to the classic way of 'score' and 'handicap' being the only judges. For example, noting where you are on the scale will again give you precious and focused feedback on how you are performing. There is no doubt in my mind that your enjoyment of the game will increase as you see those figures improve whether your handicap comes down or not. Obviously, when the scores you give to all the departments of your game start rising and you get them all at least into the better half of the scale (six-ten), your scores and handicap will follow suit. This is a far better way of getting your handicap down without you 'trying too hard.' How many times have I stood in the pro-shop on a Sunday morning listening to all the golfers who are "Going to get my handicap down today?" Of course, they are the ones with the high expectations and so it doesn't happen as they desire. The pressure they've put themselves under becomes another form of interference and their performance suffers. It's often the guy who tells you that he was out late, drank too much and got little or no sleep who then goes out with no expectations and plays a great game.

The good news is that you can learn how to let your talent show in this uninhibited manner without the need to deprive yourself of sleep or to rely on the relaxing effects of alcohol. It's just a question of increasing belief in yourself and thus releasing your inner strengths. You must trust your Self Two and your natural ability to progress through awareness.

> "I think we may safely trust a good deal more than we do"
>
> —Henry David Thoreau – American poet and writer (1817-1862)

Setting Realistic Objectives

"The name 'Positive Impact Golf' stands for coaches having a positive effect on their students, for golfers developing a more positive strike or impact on the ball, and for players to become more positive about their golf in general"

Solving Marie-Pierre's Putting Woes

LET me tell you about a woman I coached in France and the positive effect I believe that I had on her golf and how it was so simple to achieve. Let me also tell you that the speed with which she improved had a hugely positive effect on my coaching beliefs.

I had seen Marie-Pierre, a lady in her fifties and a thirty-two handicapper, about half a dozen times over a period of about six months and her swing, ball striking and general long game had improved dramatically. She was beginning to freely demonstrate the big six basics and was gaining confidence all the time. She had originally told me that putting

153

was a serious problem but had literally refused to spend any time on it at all. Usually, when someone tells me that they have a major problem I like to go straight there so as to extricate the thorn as soon as possible, so to speak.

Marie-Pierre just wouldn't get her putter out of the bag. Every time I suggested that we look at her putting she made an excuse not to do so saying that it didn't really matter and that she was happy to get to it in time. She was doing so well that, one day, I suggested that we play a few holes to see how she was taking her improvements to the course. The first hole was a fairly straightforward par four and she was delighted to hit a lovely drive with the same fluent and confident swing she had been showing on the practice range. Even more pleasing was the beautifully struck second shot she hit with a fairway wood which landed about fifty yards from the green. She had been incapable of using a wood from the fairway just a few weeks before.

She hit a nice approach shot to about fifteen feet past the flag and, as we got to the green, her whole demeanour changed when she pulled her putter from the bag. She literally started to shake with nerves. Her first putt went rushing past the hole leaving her with a twenty-footer coming back. She finally got the ball in the hole with her fifth putt. All the composure and confidence had disappeared into thin air as she literally became a nervous wreck. Now I could see why she had so systematically avoided the putter.

As we walked the hundred and fifty yards to the second tee I asked her how many putts a golfer should take on the green. "Never more than two," she replied. "Three putts are just not acceptable and I seem to do it all the time," she added with an expression on her face that couldn't hide many years of built-up anguish.

Isn't it strange? As a 32 handicap golfer we can accept that we won't hit the ball as far as a scratch player. We can accept that we won't hit as many greens in regulation, i.e. in one, two or three shots depending upon the par of the hole. We can accept much of our fate, but on the greens we don't think we should take three putts. In my mind, three putts would be much better than the five she had just taken, actually holing the last with some luck from 4 feet.

On the second hole, her tee shot was again a lovely drive followed up by another good fairway wood and a nice approach shot onto the green. Her ball was a full thirty feet from the hole and I feared for her.

I decided that she needed a more realistic goal and suggested a new objective.

"On your first putt," I proposed, "all I want you to do is greatly reduce the distance between your ball and the hole and I don't want to see the ball go past the hole. On your second putt I want you to stick the ball as close to the hole as you can without necessarily trying to hole it. Again, I don't want to see it go past the hole. Your third putt should therefore be a simple tap in."

"But that will give me three putts," she protested as she flashed me a look of total disbelief.

"Yes," I replied, "but three is much better than five, wouldn't you agree?"

"Well, yes," she said with a most unconvinced and sceptical tone in her voice and a totally unconvinced look on her face.

She took her first putt and made a much more fluid and rhythmical stroke. The ball finished two feet in front of the hole. I then repeated the mantra, "Just glue the ball to the hole without going past and don't worry about holing it."

There was a slightly bemused look on her face as the ball duly dropped in the hole. Two putts from thirty feet. Bravo!

On every green I repeated the mantra and she went from being cynical about this new idea to being completely positive about it and took only two putts per green. When we got onto the last green she found herself with a tricky fifteen foot putt where the ball was going to swing first one way then the other. I started to repeat the mantra but didn't need to finish it as she filled in the words for me. Her whole demeanour had changed dramatically and she was totally engaged in this new formula. She made another rhythmical stroke, the ball rolled smoothly off the putter, took the two borrows perfectly and popped into the hole.

"Oh! I'm sorry;" she shrieked, "I didn't mean to hole it!"

This was a perfect example of 'quick therapy' coaching in action. Her putting, both in terms of her technique and her results, had been literally revolutionised in a matter of minutes. I had identified the root cause of her putting woes and helped her resolve this without any reference whatsoever to technique.

Setting Realistic Objectives

Let's consider for a moment how traditional teaching may have been applied to her situation. It would start from the basic principle that there is something wrong so the teacher must work out what that is and put it right. The teacher looks at the physical form of her putting stroke, the exterior shell, if you like. Having seen straight away that her stroke was poor, the grip, stance, alignment, posture and swing path would all have been analysed. She would then have been told what was wrong and how to put it right. The problem with this type of teaching is that, even if it produces some improvement under the guidance of the teacher, once the player is left alone the old demons will come back and there will be no lasting cure. The enlightened coach looks beyond what can be seen and asks 'why' is she making such a complicated stroke? This is when the power of questions comes so strongly into play. Marie-Pierre's answer to my first question led me to adopt a tailored solution to her problem.

I am always keen to stress the following point to my coaches: golfers come to you with a problem but they are also the ones who possess the solution. This form of intelligent coaching not only produces quick and sustainable solutions, it also makes the job of coaching vastly more effective and enjoyable.

Timothy Gallwey, in 'The Inner Game of Tennis,' talks about 'trying hard' as being a questionable virtue. This lady was evidently trying to do something she was finding difficult and ended up trying so hard that she became overly tense about it. If only someone had told her that three putts were more than acceptable for a beginner, she would never have got into this agitated state.

The fact is that trying to do something in two that may need three, often induces tension which makes us do it in four or five. Attempting to do something in three that can be done in two will build confidence. Once confidence is installed it renders the whole affair more enjoyable and leads to success. Setting the right targets for the right person for any activity at the right time is one of the major factors in producing successful outcomes. Thus the setting of realistic, even stretching but achievable goals, can heighten motivation, an essential tool in promoting high levels of performance. If the bar is set too high or too low motivation levels tend to drop and failure can arise.

Of these two, I suggest that immediate targets that are set too high can lead to tension and failure. Long term objectives are different. I see no problem in aiming for the top as long as there is a realistic and constructive succession of minor steps leading there as well as achievable time scales.

Similarities In Business And Sport

This is as true in business as it is in sport and I remember having some difficulty persuading one of my directors that, as general manager, I felt that the budget was being set too high. The staff had suffered two changes in ownership in a short space of time and morale was low. We had failed to achieve budget in the previous year and needed to experience some success. Luckily, the other two directors supported me but this guy was very forceful and wouldn't accept anything less than the bottom line figure he wanted which I knew to be unrealistic. It was only when I used the following analogy of a dog jumping for a stick, that he finally understood my point and agreed my budget; if you hold a stick at a certain height off the ground the dog will jump for it. If you lower the stick the dog won't need to jump. If you hold it too high he won't jump either. In truth, the dog will only jump when he senses that he might be able to reach it.

Simply put, my staff had stopped jumping, but this director was worried that if the bar were set too low, everybody would get lazy. In his other businesses he always set very challenging, if not impossible targets and didn't seem to mind if they were rarely achieved. At the beginning of the year it is nice to see a healthy projected bottom line result. It keeps the directors and owners very happy. But the smiles often disappear as the month on month figures don't come up to their false expectations.

158

Ruining Kath

I have seen this happen in many business situations and, of course, many times in golf, none with more dire consequences than what happened to a young woman I was coaching in the 1980's. Kath had made fantastic progress and was playing in the British Ladies Amateur Championship in Scotland. She had played so well in this important competition that she was playing the final round in the last but one group. She literally had the chance to win it. Unfortunately, I was now working in France and wasn't in touch with her on a regular basis. She came out to see me a couple of times a year by then. A friend of hers was caddying for her all week and, enthralled by Kath's performance, tried to persuade her that she not only *could* win it but that she was *going* to win it. She persuaded Kath to wind down the car window as they drove to the course and shout at the top of her voice, "I'm going to win the British!"

Kath tried to resist. She is a lovely but, at that time, a rather shy person who was in the process of building confidence but still had some way to go. Her caddy didn't understand this and went too far. By the time she got to the first tee she was a bag of nerves. There was a delay. When her turn came to hit her drive the leaders going out in the last group had arrived on the tee and were watching. As you can imagine, these were well-known, household names and Kath felt the pressure increase. She was feeling the negative emotions of being well out of her comfort zone. She couldn't start the backswing and had to walk away from the ball and regroup. She tried again and found that the club still wouldn't move and that she now couldn't see it because she had tears in her eyes.

I won't go into any more detail as it still makes me feel angry and frustrated that this friend had put her in such a state. I can only tell you that she hit a very poor tee shot and didn't complete the round. When I saw her a few months later and she told me the story, she hadn't hit a ball since that day. Her career was seriously affected by this event and she never realised her potential. Had I been in contact with her, or had I been caddying for her, I would have told her that she had achieved a superb result even before playing the last round. I would have encouraged her to think realistically and base her day's objective on how she felt and what was comfortable for her. If she felt happy to finish in the top ten, fine. That would, in itself, have been just a wild dream when teeing up in the first round. I would have told her that she had had a successful tournament and that anything more in the last round was going to be a bonus. I would have been getting her into a state of calm wherein she could have trusted her talent and been able to enjoy the experience. As it was, she had a total nightmare that was to effectively end her career.

In this kind of situation there is great danger in thinking that it is your technique that has let you down and you start to revise and change everything you've been doing so successfully before.

> "When solving problems, dig at the roots instead of just hacking at the leaves"
>
> —Anthony J D'Angelo – Chief Visionary Officer at Collegiate Empowerment USA

Positive & Negative Boxes

"Someone once told me that people fit into two categories, radiators or drains. They either radiate positive energy or drain it from you. Your thoughts and actions work in the same way. How much energy do you radiate and how full is your positive box?"

Are You Being Positively Charged By Golf Or Is The Game Draining Your Confidence Away?

HOW many of us can honestly say that we are always positive about ourselves as golfers and about our games in general?

I believe that the inherent nature of the game and its innate inconsistency makes us all tend towards the negative side of the scale. If you are already a very positive character then you will not need to read this chapter other than to reaffirm your faith in positive energy.

When I was forming 'Positive Impact Golf' and choosing its name I was greatly influenced by the Diploma Course I had undertaken in Performance Coaching. This was a workplace-based coaching course that focused heavily on the theme of coaches having a 'positive impact' on their clients. I liked the idea of our coaches keeping this at the forefront of their minds whilst coaching and I like to feel that we are experts in helping golfers to experience a more positive impact with the ball. The better you strike the ball the stronger your self-image becomes and this in turn leads to better performances and lower scores. It also significantly increases the amount of enjoyment you will get from playing golf. I believe that one of the greatest pleasures in golf comes from the buzz of hitting the ball well.

One of the most difficult aspects of the game is the difference between the sensation of hitting a golf ball well, with its beautiful sound and awesome flight, and the dreadful feel of a bad shot with its destructive sound and disastrous flight. That topped or shanked shot that doesn't get off the ground is just soul destroying. The feeling you get when the ball soars into the sky is exciting and uplifting. Coping with these extremes is as important an aspect of the game as any other.

To recognise that you mustn't let the bad shots pull you down is essential, in my opinion, if you are to draw the most enjoyment from playing this wonderful game. Just in the same way that, when my treatment was over, I was not prepared for the ongoing effects of radiotherapy so too, if you are not prepared to hit bad shots on the golf course, you are likely to be in for a hard and frustrating time. Adopting the positive attitude of letting go of your bad shots will ensure that you hit less of them.

As Rudyard Kipling famously wrote in the poem "If" -

If you can think--and not make thoughts your aim;
If you can meet with Triumph and Disaster
And treat those two impostors just the same"

Michelle's Boxes

The term 'positive' reminds me of an idea I had come up with many years ago whilst coaching in France. I'd like to share this true story with you now.

Michelle, a lady in her late thirties who wasn't a member of the club where I was coaching, turned up for her first session with me and appeared to be a rather unsmiling and serious character. When I asked what had brought her to book a lesson with me she explained that she was a beginner whose husband was a keen golfer and wanted her to share his passion. She had tried to learn twice before and had hated it! She now had a pact with her husband that she would try a third and last time and then he would stop pestering her about playing golf and leave her to be a happy golf widow. Her husband had heard about me and booked the session for her. She added that she was useless at golf and couldn't ever see herself enjoying it. As you can imagine, this was not the ideal recipe for an enthusiastic and fun-filled golf lesson.

Anyway, she hit a few balls with a seven-iron and to my surprise she hit the ball quite well and had a reasonably good swing. When I shared this with her it seemed to make no difference to her state of mind; she obviously had a very negative opinion of herself and the game of golf. I felt that I needed to get something positive going or it was going to be an unhappy experience for both of us.

163

I began by asking her to say something positive after each shot. She could only continue to make negative and self-degrading comments. So, I told her that she would hit the shots and I would do the positive comments. Her next shot went straight towards the target, up in the air, not particularly well struck, but flew about sixty yards.

Before I could say a word she said, "Well that's pretty awful!"

I told her that I begged to differ as I found it not bad at all considering the little she had played the game. She wasn't convinced, especially when her next shot went thirty yards along the ground.

"There's nothing good to say about that one either, is there?"

"It went straight," I replied.

"Oh, you are positive, aren't you?"

I explained that, whilst I endeavour to be as positive as possible, there is no future in me kidding her, or her kidding herself for that matter, and that I was only seeing things as they were whereas I felt that she was being unduly hard on herself. She admitted that she was generally a rather negative person in life anyway and so this was only her normal way of operating. That's when the box idea came to my mind.

Pointing to the ground to her right, I told her to imagine a box which was labelled 'positive' and then pointed to her left, indicating that here was another box which was labelled 'negative'.

"The problem as I see it," I explained, "is that every time you make a comment, or react to something, you put a token in one of the boxes depending on whether it's a positive or negative reaction. You probably don't realise it but your negative box is full and very heavy whilst your positive one is empty and light. The negative one is dragging you down. To get a better balance you need to start putting some tokens in the positive box. All I am trying to do is highlight the good rather than focus on the bad. I am not asking you to lie to yourself about how you are doing."

We continued in this vein for the rest of the first session and continued to do likewise in the second. Gradually she became more at ease with the idea and started to gain confidence.

I was chipping a few balls as I waited for her to arrive for her third session and suddenly heard a loud and enthusiastic "Bonjour!" coming from behind me. I turned to find a bright and cheerful Michelle bouncing towards me with a charming smile on her face.

"Well," she said. "Haven't you noticed?"

"I'm sorry," I said. "I can see that you appear happy to be here today, which I am delighted about but, apart from that, I'm not quite sure what you mean."

Pointing to her right, she proudly announced "Voila, the positive box." She then looked to her left and seemed confused as if she had lost something.

"Oh dear," she exclaimed, "I must have left the negative box at home!"

"Bravo, Michelle. You have fully understood the message!"

Now, I can't honestly tell you that she went on to win the club championship or become a scratch golfer as I left the area shortly afterwards, but I know that she had a chance of playing an enjoyable game of golf with her husband. She had also helped me to identify a simple mental image that can help anyone who needs a boost of positive energy.

Remember Tim Gallwey's words? "The way you do something is the way you do anything." I would like to think that Michelle's golf lessons helped her to a more positive attitude in other areas of her life.

How Positive Are You?

On a scale of zero to ten where are you in terms of being positive? How would your golfing life be if you took that score up a few points? If you registered anything from six to ten you are, at least, in the upper half. Say you are at seven it would obviously help your game if you were to improve to an eight or a nine. If you are under six and in the lower half, you can make a significant step forward and start to enjoy your golf more without any need to change your swing or practice more. Just get a few more tokens in your positive box and you'll see and feel the difference in no time. I recently read an article about the brain's power to fully integrate change that explained that it takes 21 days for the process to be completed. The challenge is to keep this new attitude for just three weeks.

Why don't you start that notebook that I told you about earlier? You know, the one in which you record all your good shots? Go on. Do it now! Make it a rule to write down anything positive that happens to you in golf. You must record at least the three best shots of every round. If you've had a bad day, then write down the three least bad shots of the day. Over a period of time you will be surprised at what you will have recorded. You will be able to remember the feeling of those good shots for a long, long time afterwards. The positive effect will stay with you for as long as you keep the notebook. Remember, three weeks is a minimum for it to start working effectively.

When I first met John he was one of the stiffest and most tense players I had ever met. He would regularly hit several baskets of balls and leave looking frustrated and exhausted. Just a few days ago he was practicing at the range. In the bay next to him was a golfer he didn't know. As golfers do, they got into conversation and the guy told John that he had never seen anyone hit the ball so well with so little effort and asked how he did it. This was more than music to John's ears and he wrote it down in his notebook as soon as he got home.

Do you remember Raymond and the sign that invited employees to come to see him armed with solutions not problems? You can adopt the same philosophy whenever you want to in your golf game.

As a General Manager I always tried to follow the same theme and ask my department heads to seek their own solutions. After all, I was only a "general" manager whereas they were specialists in their own areas. My role was more involved with discussing, facilitating and rubber-stamping their decisions not in doing their jobs for them. I wonder how many people are capable of truly empowering their staff and how many just pay lip service to the idea?

Do you remember that I promised to demonstrate how you could benefit more fully from your personal capabilities? A simple combination of using this notebook and filling your positive box will empower you to identify areas of potential improvement whilst helping you to build added confidence in your own ability. It is not only an uncomplicated system but it also will lead to better golf without resorting to technical and complex modifications with all the 'hard work' and effort that this requires.

A couple of weeks after Paul Casey holed a four-iron in the 2006 Ryder Cup at the K Club in Ireland he was talking about it to a journalist. He immediately stated that this shot was already recorded in his 'best shot' notebook. Although I would normally advise against copying the tour pros, this is one example where, if it works for Paul, it can work for you.

Do You Know Your Distances?

Let me tell you about another area where we golfers take the wrong route to better golf.

One day, I was playing a few holes with a lady who had only just got her first handicap. We were on the first of the golf school holes, a short par four of three hundred yards, and she had a third shot of around fifty yards to the green.

"How far is the pin," she asked me?

"Why do you ask," I responded?

"Because my husband tells me that I should know my distances."

Her answer didn't surprise me as husbands often give their wives this kind of advice.

The ground in front of her was flat and there were no obstacles in the way. It was not, in my opinion, of any use to her to know what the exact distance was. The shot was, in any case, an intermediate not a full approach shot and feel for the distance was more important than actual distance knowledge. Instead of explaining all this I asked her to throw a ball at a nearby tree which was about twelve paces away. She made a nice swinging movement and the ball landed a yard from the tree.

"How far is the tree," I asked?

"Oh, about twenty yards," she said.

So we paced it out and it was, in fact, thirteen yards. She immediately understood that judgement of distance has little to do with your brain knowing or calculating how far it is. It starts, in my opinion, with your eyes feeding the information to the brain and then leaving your sense of feel to sort out the intricacies of how much force is required. Yes, the choice of club is important but please bear in mind that there are usually several clubs that can do the job. Top players will take time to choose which club and which way to play that club for a particular shot, but they are much more experienced in the art and added information about distance can be very helpful. For most of us, however, we would do better just to let our instincts and intuition stay in charge instead of letting the calculating side of the brain get too involved.

When you drive a vehicle and you are approaching a bend do you need to know how far away from it you should be when you start to brake? Do you think about the speed you are travelling at and then calculate the exact moment to apply the brakes? Do you think about how much pressure is required on the pedal? Of course not! If you did you'd probably never get round the first bend. The act of driving a vehicle makes for an interesting comparison with playing golf. The two activities are very similar in the learning stages but it doesn't take long to assimilate all the salient points about driving a vehicle and it soon becomes a bit like riding a bike. It becomes something you'll probably never forget how to do. So, why, in the world of golf do we have so much difficulty getting the same result? Because we don't put the learning stage behind us, even gradually, and we are constantly toying with even the most basic elements of how to play the game. In reality, we never take the 'L' plates off.

'Positive Impact Golf' achieves high levels of success because it is based on the golfer's natural ability not only to learn, but also to perform the task of swinging a club and hitting a ball. It is, as Ernest Jones said all those years ago, really quite a simple task. Have we, the golf teachers, conspired to make it unnatural, complex, complicated and difficult? I leave you to answer this question yourself.

"Our spontaneous action is always the best. You cannot, with your best deliberation and heed, come so close to any question as your spontaneous glance shall bring you"

—Ralph Waldo Emerson – American Essayist, Poet & Philosopher (1803-1882)

Why We Top The Ball

> "If there's one expression that I would like to banish from the language of golfers, it is "YOU LIFTED YOUR HEAD"

What Topping Can Do To You

DO you know a golfer who has never 'topped' a ball? Do you know anyone who didn't completely miss the ball occasionally the first few times they had a go? I have seen a few but they are certainly a rare breed. I know I missed the odd ball and topped my fair share of shots when I started to play.

Most people are particularly sensitive to what they do and to what happens to them when they commence a new activity. In golf, our first attempts are often less than fantastic. Debilitating negative self-images start invading our minds at this early and vulnerable stage.

Making a fool of yourself in front of your friends and colleagues is not likely to fill you with enthusiasm for the game! In fact, at that time, it bears no resemblance to a 'game' at all and can be quite demoralising. I wonder how many prospective golfers ever make it past this initial meeting with the intricacies of hitting a little innocent and inoffensive ball. Now, I might be exaggerating but my comments are based on some factual experience. Just last week I coached two different ladies on the same afternoon who will both play much better golf when they accept that they are normally gifted at it and not as useless as they think. They are in their sixties and play off twenty-seven and thirty-five handicaps. Both used the following term to describe how they feel on the course when hitting a bad shot, "I feel so stupid." Yet they are very intelligent, successful women who swing the club quite well but suffer from a lack of confidence. They are far from being stupid.

Knowing their negative self-images, can you imagine how they react to playing in front of other golfers? Are they likely to move freely with an air of authority or are they more likely to look a little shy and make inhibited and nervous movements? The answer is that they will find great improvement in their shots when they have the confidence to move MORE. With the aid of 'La Danse du Golf' both ladies are making good progress and are already displaying more of the six basic elements. What they both need is the confidence to make those better swings when they play on the course with other players. They both now understand the effects of Timothy Gallwey's Self One and Self Two inner conversations and are gradually learning to trust their Self Two's. They are also filling their positive boxes and letting go of the negative ones just as Michelle did so successfully.

The first hurdle to get over when you start to play this game is to know that your ball will consistently get off the ground. When you stand over every shot with the feeling that you are likely to hit it well and get it up in the air your confidence will grow. Whilst it is likely that beginners will top the ball quite regularly, there is no reason why this shouldn't disappear after a while. Now, this may be a few weeks or a few months and it is important to know that even pros can top the odd one.

What Really Causes Topping

Let's have a closer look at how a golf ball is topped. The word 'topped' is significant because it means that the club has contacted the top of the ball. If the club doesn't contact the ball under its centre-line or equator it won't fly up in the air. There are 3 major causes of this problem:

1. **Tension in hands and arms.** Try the following experiment. Hold a 7-iron at your side with the head of the club touching the ground beside your feet. You should hold it very lightly and your arm should hang loosely with your shoulder low and relaxed. Now, see what happens when your hand tightens on the grip and your arm and shoulder stiffen with this effort. The club comes off the ground! Have you lifted your head? No.

2. **Your head comes up but not because it moved in an effort to look up early.** Why would you do that? After all, the main focus is on hitting the ball so why would you be looking anywhere else? No, the whole body has been forced up because its natural path through the shot has been blocked by the intention to keep your head down. Your golfing partners see your head coming up because we are all obsessed by the head in golf. What they don't see is the whole body moving up, the weight not moving forward and your legs straightening. Top golfers keep their centre of gravity at a constant height until well after impact. Top golfers don't try to keep their heads down. In all the years I've played tournament golf I've *never* heard a fellow pro tell

173

another player that he lifted his head! Tony Jacklin was interviewed on Radio 5 Live shortly after his book was published in 2008. He was asked what was the worst tip he'd ever been given. He didn't hesitate in answering, "Keep my head down!"

3. The distance between your body's centre and the club head is too short to pick up the bottom of the ball because you have un-cocked your wrists too late as you approach impact. You will remember the troubles I suffered by working hard on the 'late hit.' Well, I even got to the stage where my 3-wood tee shots were often topped and could shoot off at right angles. Most embarrassing for a young tournament player!

Please bear in mind that you don't have to hit down to get the ball flying. All you need is the club to be low enough to get under the centre of the ball, i.e. the equator of the ball, and that it is moving forward at some speed. Personally, I rarely ask players to hit down as this concept produces the wrong type of movement that will compromise your ability to turn freely through the shot and finish the movement correctly. I will talk to you later in this chapter about the importance of finishing the golf swing well.

In over 30 years of studying videos and watching average golfers I have rarely seen anyone topping the ball because they looked up too early. The only players I've seen let their heads turn early are several pros and low handicap amateurs and it doesn't stop them hitting great shots consistently.

Tension is generally at the core of most ills in golf and nowhere is this more damaging than when it gets into your muscles and joints. When we concentrate too much, or concentrate in the wrong way, tension often creeps into the shoulders. I'm sure you've experienced this when driving your car or concentrating on the computer screen and have to lower and relax them from time to time. In golf, tension stiffens and shortens our muscles and leads to topping, shanking, i.e. hitting the ball off the heel of an iron, and general excesses in the effort required to hit the ball.

As a fault it is one of the most devious as it doesn't always show itself to the spectator. Two swings may look identical, even under the magnifying glass of slow motion and still frame video images, but hidden tension can make one of them top the ball whilst the other can produce a great shot.

The Head Down Brigade

Now, it is easy to understand where the 'Head Down Brigade' get their ideas from. They are the scientists who apply simple but erroneous geometry to the art of hitting a golf ball. Most of us are willingly led down this path as we look for the 'secret of golf' that will cure us from bad shots for ever. The thinking goes as follows:

"If I keep my head absolutely still and retain the same radius of circle via a straight left arm and limit any other bodily movement to the bare minimum I can't fail to hit the ball properly."

Well, you might hit it but you won't display many of the basics we have talked about earlier in the book. How will you create good rotation and weight transfer? How will you achieve good rhythm? How can you, at one and the same time, keep large parts of your body static and stay synchronised with other parts that are now called upon to do the Trojan's share of the work? Surely everything needs to move and coordinate together if we are going to get anywhere near playing consistent golf?

You might also think that keeping your feet glued firmly to the ground whilst limiting the size your movement will lead to better balance. You would be wrong. This way of making a golf swing doesn't understand the 'dynamics' of movement and often leads to players finishing with their weight on the wrong foot. Combined with the idea of keeping your head still this will push your weight onto the wrong foot at the end of your back swing. This is called a 'reverse pivot' and is one of the worst faults you can have.

Obviously, when someone tops a ball something is wrong. The club must have hit the top of the ball. Logically, the player must have lifted up and sometimes you'd be right to think so. But your head doesn't come up independently. It only comes up because the whole body lifts up and certainly not because you have looked up before you hit it. I have been studying golf swings for over forty years and have been filming golfers of all standards for over thirty years. The fact is that it is only very good players who have the confidence to take their eyes off the ball before they hit it. Most of us have been too indoctrinated to think that it is vital to keep our eyes on the ball, or are so ball conscious, to ever look anywhere else.

Great golfers such as Annika Sorenstam, David Duval, Henrik Stenson, Robert Allenby and Paul Azinger are just a few who are showing us the way forward. I confidently predict that you will see more and more players adopting this technique in the future. Remember, the ball doesn't move until we hit it so it's not like a moving ball game. By the time your club reaches a point even a couple of feet before impact it's too late to change where it's going to pass so why stare at the ball as if it's going to suddenly run off and escape the committed and soon to arrive club head.

The truth is that if we act as if the ball is going to run off before we hit it we become its prisoner. The fear of moving in case we completely mess up the shot or miss it altogether is the emotion controlling our actions!

Make Sure You Don't Mistake Why Your Game Has Deteriotated

My sister, Brenda, sent her friend, Nabil, to see me from his home in Switzerland. He is in his late sixties and loves his golf. However, he was struggling with his game and, in particular, couldn't get through to any sort of full finish. He had been diagnosed with Alzheimer's disease a short time ago and thought that this, plus the ageing process in general, was the cause of his problem. After all, everyone told him that his club stopped shortly after impact and he felt it on virtually every shot. His brain just couldn't seem to get the message through to his body about finishing the swing.

I asked him a few questions and his answers were in line with traditional thinking. He was trying to keep his head down, his eye on the ball and was trying to hold the club on a straight line to the target for as long as possible after impact. He was also trying to keep his arms straight after impact.

With the positive effects of 'La Danse du Golf' and a short time working on a relaxed finish position, his swing improved and he achieved a full and balanced end to his swing. Where had the Alzheimer's effect gone? Of course, this debilitating disease is never going to make it easy to play golf but the plain truth is that this man was going to give up on golf because of the old beliefs he was unwittingly and subconsciously trying to conform to. The worse he played the more he applied them! Over two one-hour sessions his swing improved tenfold and he hit the ball further than for a long time.

I refuse to get sad and frustrated when I see so many people in the older age group suffering so needlessly in this way. I prefer to use my emotions to fuel my desire to do something about it and hence this book.

177

Age Need Not Be The Barrier
You Think It Is

In the last year alone 'Positive Impact Golf' has helped many senior golfers including Jill and Bryan to revise their thoughts about giving the game up in their 60's. Jill was so unhappy with her golf that she had decided that enough was enough. Not only is she now enjoying her golf more than ever before, her driver has become the strongest club in her game whereas she hadn't used a wood for 10 years. Bryan, a long time scratch golfer now playing off fourteen, was desperately looking to achieve the natural swing he had been seeking since turning fifty when his game started to deteriorate. Bill won a trophy at his club and had his handicap reduced from 20 to 18 at the age of 78 and having had two knee replacements. It has helped so many others that I won't bore you with the details but suffice it to say that they are many and of all differing levels and abilities. They share a rejuvenation of their game and increased enjoyment of golf that makes coaching so rewarding.

On the other side of the coin, 'Positive Impact Golf' currently has a group of youngsters who are benefiting from the same easier swing techniques. I have great hopes for them in the coming years. I believe that golfers tend to reach their peak at somewhere around thirty-five to forty years of age, a frightening fact for Tiger Woods' current opponents. We coach hundreds of kids and see many amongst them who will become fine players. The long term future for these golfers is very rosy and setting them on a simple and natural path is essential. So, too, is protecting them from the negative effects of the classic restrictions of head down, stiff arms and limited footwork. However, it's the adult and senior golfer who has a more pressing need of this more natural way of playing the game.

If you are a senior lady or a senior gentleman, please let us help you. Please look closely at the philosophy in this book and ask yourself, "Do I want to carry on with deteriorating golf? Do I want to accept that I can't hit it like I used to?"

Now, I'm not promising you an extra fifty yards on your drives, although this does happen to some golfers whose swings have become very restricted. No, but what you can get is an extension to the years of playing enjoyable golf and that alone is worth looking at. Remember Henry? He's like a dog with two tails and it didn't take long. You are vastly more life-experienced than young people and, despite what other people think and tell you, I know that you can learn quickly and easily. The fact is that you need to move your feet more freely to make up for the stiffening joints and the lack of natural flexibility. You, more than anyone, need to let your head move with your body. All you need is an open mind with a positive attitude towards your ability to change and a bit of belief in yourself and you can achieve remarkable progress.

All these people and many others have been highly instrumental in showing me just how important it is for senior golfers to break with the old-fashioned basics. Do you recall the members at Barton-on-Sea? They couldn't turn like they used to. I agree that age does stiffen the joints and that your muscles and tendons lose much of their flexibility. At 58 I'm feeling the effects of age as much as anyone but my golf swing doesn't show it as I allow myself to play in a very relaxed manner and, although I can't dance like Fred Astaire, I feel much of 'la souplesse' that younger and more supple players display.

The good news is that you can keep turning more fully as long as you use more footwork and allow your head to move naturally with your body. Of course, any amount of trying to keep your arms straight and extended or coiling like a spring in the back swing will add tension and difficulty to your swing and make your golfing life unpleasant and ineffective.

"Age is opportunity, no less,
Than youth itself, though in another dress,
And as the evening twilight fades away,
The sky is filled with stars, invisible by day"

—Henry Wadsworth Longfellow –
American Poet (1807-1882) from
Morituri Salutamus

The Importance of Finishing Well

"One of Buddhism's core beliefs is that something will bear fruit if it is good at the beginning, good in the middle and good at the end. The way you finish your golf shots has a major effect on how you prepare for and how you perform the main part of your swing. Ignore it at your peril"

Does It Matter What Happens After The Ball Leaves The Club Face?

ONE of the most influential and damaging beliefs is that it doesn't matter what happens in the swing after the ball has been struck. After all, how can this have any effect on the ball? Well, let's have a closer look at this essential part of the swing.

If Martin, my very first assistant golf pro, ever reads the following passage, he will think it's been written by someone else. He tried to persuade me over thirty years ago that the end of the swing was highly important. At that time, I was greatly into the technique of posture and positional golf. I thought then that achieving good positions, both at the address and at the top of the back swing, was essential if the goal of consistently good shots was to be achieved. Remember, this was the period when I was trying to solve my problems with technical solutions. How wrong I was to look outside my box instead of reverting back to what was already inside me!

In his book 'Psycho-Cybernetics' Dr. Maxwell Maltz quotes a hypnotist who stated that...."Clients visit me hoping that I will put them in a trance and fix their lives. In fact many of them live in a trance and need a dose of reality."

Psycho-Cybernetics sounds intimidating and technical but is, in fact, a simple philosophy regarding the power of our self-image to control our lives. Dr. Maltz, a plastic surgeon, wrote his book in 1960 after discovering that many of his clients looked better after an operation but failed to benefit from the improvements because their self-image was incapable of letting go of its habitual picture. In the story of my own golf, my reality (self-image) was that my technique was flawed. When, despite years of practice, analysis and swing refinement, my game and scores failed to show any substantial improvement I was left with a self-image that was worse than before the process began. If my technique was good then I must be innately incapable.

Sam Snead once wrote "I've seen a lot of good positions with awful swings and I've seen a lot of awful positions with great swings." How right he was! The technical approach was very attractive to me as I was fully signed up to the 'culture of golfers.' Something was wrong and I needed to find out what it was and fix it.

In point no. 8 I told you about the club head reaching its maximum speed well after impact. Combine this concept with the knowledge that good shots are the result of releasing the club fully and freely through the ball and you can begin to see just how important it is to finish well. How can you accelerate through your shots if the club is slowing down or stopping at the very point where it should be at its greatest speed? Achieving good ball striking involves two very basic elements. Firstly you must be relaxed, as your muscles and joints need maximum elasticity and flexibility to work at speed, just in the same way that you would find it difficult to crack a whip with stiff muscles and joints. Secondly, there must be a positive intent even on the smallest of shots. Failing to complete the movement to its required end, whether on a full shot, a half shot or even a short putt, is simply guaranteed to reduce your chances of consistent and sustainable success.

Photo 15   Photo 16

Take a look at photo 15. This is what I believe to be the sort of comfortable position you should be looking for. Note Greg's vertical spine, the relaxed and folded arms and the position of his head.

His shoulders and arms are low and there is plenty of space between his right ear and right shoulder. Not how much his body has turned and how much shoulder rotation he has achieved. Now, as I've said before, I don't believe in over-emphasis on positions as that can have a negative effect on motion and your mind will be focused on what different parts of your body are doing instead of thinking of the feel of the movement as a whole. But, the feel of the end of your swing can help you to achieve better and more fluid strokes as well as ensuring against back pain from twisted, unnatural, ungainly and unbalanced finishes. A good finish is one of the common points amongst good golfers, not that they all look the same but they do generally finish in balance and look composed, hardly what you would see in the majority of amateur players.

Photo 16 shows Greg demonstrating the sort of position that you can see every day anywhere golf is played. This was, indeed, how he used to swing the club. Note the high and tense right shoulder, the high hands, the limited rotation of his body and the tension in his back. When taking into account that most of us fall into the trap of forcing our shots and replacing relaxed movement with pure effort, it isn't too difficult to see how much pressure he is putting on his body. Imagine hitting 100 balls at the driving range with this finish position on every shot? It's just like receiving a thump in the back at the end of every shot. Also worth noting is the fact that his shoulders have turned further than the traditional 'facing the target' position often advised to the average golfer. This is indicative of the amount of rotation seen in better golf swings and is only possible if your head moves freely through the shot and your arms are allowed to fold early after impact.

Photo 17 shows young Noah in the sort of awkward position that even someone of his age will produce with the old ideas of head down and high hands. Photo 20 shows a more relaxed, comfortable and composed end to his swing.

I have seen many youngsters suffer from bad backs or get disillusioned by the discomfort of playing golf in the old ways. As he develops I will be encouraging him to turn more fully but will ask him to keep his arms nicely connected to his body action.

Another major misconception which inhibits your ability to achieve a good and full finish is that your leading arm should stay as straight as possible for as long as possible after impact. For a right-handed player this only serves to block the release of the right side through the ball. It is completely acceptable to allow your leading arm to fold naturally so that your club can continue to accelerate through the shot.

Photo 17   Photo 18

It is totally within your ability to achieve a better and more relaxed finish position. It is one of the most powerful tools for enabling golfers to radically improve their game and yet sadly, is terribly underestimated by many golf coaches. I know. I was one of them.

Obstacles To Finishing Well

There are other notable obstacles to getting through to a good finish such as paying too much attention to the ball and the target, both of which can act as blocking factors. The destination of the club head on a full shot is roughly down one's back. When starting the down swing, this, not the ball or target, should be your objective and you should have pre-set yourself by feel to get there whatever the impact with the ball might be.

The concept of keeping your head down as you strike the ball along with the idea of keeping your arms extended towards the target will combine to make it nearly impossible to reach your objective of a composed, relaxed and full finish. It will also severely compromise your chances of releasing the club freely through the ball at speed, something that the best players achieve more consistently than other players, whatever their individual swing characteristics may be.

When you regularly achieve a full finish and release the club with acceleration even your bad shots will go further and straighter.

To help you achieve this I strongly recommend that you hold your finish position until the ball stops rolling. The benefits of this simple piece of advice are threefold:

1. You will have the time to feel how you have just performed the shot thus giving immediate and useful feedback.
2. You can instantly correct anything resulting from this feedback, e.g. balance, shoulder tension, weight transfer. Although not

helping the shot you've just hit, this correction will serve to remind you of the feel of the end you should be achieving.

3.   You'll know where to look for your ball!

As I said before about your reaction to bad shots, if you feel or sense immediately what went wrong, then by all means use the information in a positive way. But, if you don't feel it straight away and don't know why you've messed up, do nothing. Just put a cross against it and walk off to the next shot and do your best the next time. You can also use the time between shots to shed all the negativity of the poor shot and get yourself into the right state to perform well on the next one. If you are practicing and hit one or several bad shots, make sure you take a few minutes off to recollect yourself and your thoughts.

In 'Zen Golf' Dr Parent advises us to say something like, *"Hmmm. Interesting,"* or, *"How unlike me,"* which will at least get a laugh from your playing partners.

Having studied many golfers practicing on ranges and practice grounds around the world over many years I am convinced they hit too many balls too quickly, especially when it starts to go wrong. Not only can this lead to increased frustration but fails to mirror the rhythm of the game on the course where you usually have a few minutes between shots.

There is one aspect to finishing well that is deceptive. You will be so relaxed that the power element will feel quite low. You will, however, be amazed as to how long the ball stays in flight and how far it flies. At first, you will not believe it. Our coaches often tell me about the "Aha" moment when this happens to a client for the first time. I can assure you that it is a regular occurrence in our sessions with golfers of all levels. People are usually expending enormous but uneconomic amounts of energy in hitting a golf ball. Remember the young French woman who couldn't even manage to play a full round of golf? Let me explain my thoughts which differ from more traditional views.

Effort And Energy

When you swing a golf club you are creating energy; you are like a human dynamo. When the amount of effort is excessive and ill-directed, only a small amount of it gets to the ball. The player experiences a net loss of energy as most of what he or she has produced evaporates into thin air. The net result is disappointing and frustrating. Effort and reward don't add up. When you increase elasticity and free up more movement, the effort and strain reduces and you create more energy and speed. There is more potential energy available to release into the ball. But, here is the surprise factor, some of it stays in you. Not only do you hit the ball further but you also feel less drained of energy. A practice session like this will leave you feeling energised but relaxed and calm. Add to this the feeling of a balanced, composed yet full follow through and you will not only enjoy hitting the ball better and further, but you will also enjoy swinging the club to the full and we all know that this is a beautiful feeling.

As you come to recognise the new sensations of a good finish you will realise that knowing how you are going to end your swing leads instinctively and even unconsciously to getting the preparation and middle parts right. As George said to me one day whilst we were focusing on his finish position on mid-distance pitch shots, "Right, then. If I should end up in a more relaxed finish position then I need to be more relaxed as I address the ball." He was absolutely right and discovered this gem of information entirely on his own. He had helped himself to a more relaxed and successful way of playing all his pitches. Teachers and coaches please take note; I didn't tell him what to do. I just acted as a catalyst in helping him to discover something himself.

This philosophy of how people learn best is at the core of my values in 'Positive Impact Golf.' It is easier to coach, easier to learn and, most fundamentally, much more likely to be retained and progressed further by the student because he found it and didn't have it imposed on him. When you feel that you've discovered something yourself but it doesn't work all the time you are far more likely to persevere whereas, when you've simply been told what to do you, will probably revert to your old way the moment it doesn't appear to be working. You'll think of it as just another idea that didn't work. Helping people to discover things for themselves is a major factor in golfers improving faster and in a more sustainable way than with traditional instruction.

> "Alice came to a crossroads with several roads leading from it. Feeling lost, she asked the Cat which one she should take. 'Where are you going,' asked the Cat? 'It doesn't much matter,' said Alice. 'Then it doesn't much matter which road you take,' replied the cat!"
>
> —Lewis Carroll – Alice in Wonderland

How My Game Has Developed

"Once I learnt how to really relax and to rid myself of the obsession for the mechanics of the golf swing, I found capabilities I thought I didn't possess"

BEFORE I summarise the content of 'Positive Impact Golf' I should tell you how my own game progressed. You will remember that I played promising golf as a beginner because I somehow knew what to do without knowing how I was doing it. When I learnt classic and traditional methods my game became more difficult and I didn't know how to play anymore. I then sought technical solutions to my problems, never thinking that a return to natural golf would have been a wiser option.

Well, I continued in the mechanical mode for many years until two things happened. Firstly, I could see the progress of my students as they were released from the 'paralysis by analysis' syndrome. I have always been very self-critical as a coach and began to see and feel the positive and sometimes amazing results that were happening as my coaching moved away from mechanics and positions. This served as a motivating factor in letting go of old beliefs and trusting more in movement in my own game.

Secondly, I met Michel, but before I tell you about his influence on my game let me explain how it came about.

Winning My Card

A couple of years after my move to France, I competed in a 36-hole regional open championship which was played on a very long modern course with the fastest, biggest and most undulating greens I'd ever come across. I did well and got a surge of confidence that led me to seek some help in my aim to play a few tournaments on the French circuit. I instinctively knew that I needed to develop my mental game.

I had hit the ball very poorly in my practice round but experience told me that the tournament would be won and lost on the greens so, whilst all the other competitors hit the usual amount of balls on the practice range, I set up camp on the putting green. I eventually succeeded in getting my rhythm to a very quiet level where my touch became quite delicate. By the time I got onto the first tee I was able to attack any putt with an accelerating club head whilst still controlling the distance. Even on fast greens you must still strike the ball positively. The club must accelerate into the ball.

In the first round I hit the ball well enough from tee to green to benefit from some good putting and finished tied for the lead. On the second day I hit the ball a bit more solidly and continued to putt well, recording sixty-three putts over the two rounds, about a dozen less than the average. I was beaten into second place by a young and highly successful tour player but was delighted to think that the result wasn't bad for a thirty-eight-year-old coach who had little or no time to play or practice. Whilst I knew that I wasn't competing against the same standard of player I had played against on the European Tour sixteen years earlier, it still gave my confidence a real boost and I decided to go for my card for the French circuit in the qualifying tournament to be held a couple of months later.

I prepared strongly, not so much in actual play but with a bit of practice between coaching sessions and going to the gym three or four times a week to get me feeling good about myself. My self-image had been weakened by my previous tournament attempts but a regime of weight training and running boosted the seed of confidence that came with the good result I had just recorded. But, just two weeks before the six-round event for my card, disaster struck as I went down with a severe appendicitis and was operated on in urgency.

By this time I had married my second wife, Fabienne, and her father, a physiotherapist, immediately advised that my attempt to gain my card would have to wait twelve months as in no way would I be able to play serious golf for a month or so. But I love a challenge so set myself the task of succeeding against the odds. After a few days in hospital, I went home with the surgeon's words firmly in my mind: "Your stitches will hold together and, as long as you wait a few days and don't do anything strenuous at first, there is no medical reason why you can't play your tournament."

So, with the family completely against this mad Englishman's idea of competing two weeks after the operation, off I went. I limped off the course after nine holes of the practice round and was struggling to play any form of decent shots. I made the choice of a light ladies, shortened-shaft twelve-degree graphite shaft driver and, in any case, I had already changed to graphite shafts in my irons for their flexibility so hadn't any problem using this to make up for the limitations of my injury.

I finished the first round in sixth place and hung on to win my card quite comfortably despite tough weather, a course in very poor condition and quite a lot of discomfort. This taught me a salutary lesson. You don't need to hit the ball hard to play good golf. It also confirmed that, in order to play without stressing my injury, I had to move my feet even more than ever before. Abandoning any traces of the traditional coil/torsion type of swing made it possible for me to play six competitive rounds in eight days.

What The Heck Is A Relaxologue/ Sophrologiste?

When I got home I spent some time reflecting on how I would coordinate playing some tournaments with my life as a coach and decided that I would work for three weeks and then take a week off to play a tournament. This would give me approximately six tournaments over the following season. Having decided to get serious with the mental side of the game I found the name of Michel Perroux, a 'relaxalogue / sophrologiste', in the local 'pages jaunes' (yellow pages). Sophrologie is translated as 'relaxation therapy.'

When we first met he explained that, though he had never played golf and knew little about it, he could undoubtedly help me to improve my performances. Our first session lasted two hours and he sent me away to reflect on my objectives for the coming year and for the two following years also. What a shock to my system and what a difficult task it turned out to be. I was the sort of person who tended to just go with life's flow and never looked more than a couple of weeks ahead. Of course, looking back, he was giving the same advice to me that the Cat gave to

Alice. If you don't know where you're going, how can you make all the micro-decisions that you will undoubtedly be required to make if you are to succeed? It is exactly the same in any part of life be it in sport, in business or in your personal affairs.

Using My Natural Intuition

I visited Michel regularly and he helped me to achieve the best standard of golf I had ever reached. He didn't know anything about golf but he soon identified simple and powerful ways to make me more positive and thus let more of my potential show through. He watched me play and encouraged me to make more use of my natural intuition. In one tournament round I was on the cusp of making the halfway cut when my second shot missed the green by a few yards on the short par four, fifteenth hole. When I got to my ball I was delighted to see that it was lying perfectly for a little nine-iron chip and run, my favourite shot at that time. I went to my bag to get my club but it refused to come out and the eight-iron seemed to be shouting at me instead. I went back to have another look at the shot and returned to my bag further convinced that it was the perfect nine-iron situation. Again my eight-iron called. It was like it was a young child saying "Take me, take me; please take me."

I went back a third time and, again, was totally happy with the nine-iron option. Again the eight called but this time I heard Michel's voice telling me to trust my intuition. I took the eight-iron and, lo and behold, holed out for a birdie. I went on to pass the cut quite comfortably.

Here was real evidence of that conversation between 'me' and 'myself,' between my Self One and my Self Two. Luckily, and with Michel's help, I listened to my gut instincts which knew more about what was going on than did my conscious mind and Self Two won the day. It is a wonderful but mysterious thing that we can achieve great success without being able to describe how we did it. The fact that we find it difficult to trust our instincts leads us to mistrust them and so we go with the advice of the ever present and talkative Self One. I can only say, 'do so at your own peril.'

I had successes on the golf course that I had only dreamed of including stretches of sustained low scoring, something I had always found difficult before. I used to get nervous as the good holes mounted up and the feeling that it couldn't last would eventually get to me. My self-image was stronger than ever before and produced a period of play that was by far the most technique-free of my whole life.

I carried on seeing Michel for many years and he also proved massively helpful in the evolution of my coaching beliefs and, later on, in my foray into the world of management. I owe him the greatest gratitude for passing his knowledge on to me.

Many years later I discovered 'Zen Golf' by Dr Joseph Parent. I can recommend this book as one of the best I've ever read as you will find jewels of advice on the mental aspect of golf on every page. He talks about 'anyway' shots where you go on and hit the ball despite the feeling that something isn't quite right. He advises us to note them when it happens so that, over time, we will recognise them and be able to stop before making the mistake of hitting the shot when our intuition is telling us not to. The story of my 8-iron chip shot demonstrates how I may well have hit a poor chip if I had hit it 'anyway' with my favourite 9-iron.

The Consequences Of Traditional Basics
Finally Catch Up With Me

I was born with a fused lowest lumber vertebra and, eventually, the disc above gave out under the strain of all those years of hitting balls with my head down and working on the wide variety of 'methods' which came into fashion during my technical years. Those of you of a certain age will remember the 'square-to-square' and 'reverse C' doctrines. In 1997 at the age of 46 I had a back operation that effectively ended my playing career. I now enjoy playing about once a month and play with little or no thought. I play naturally and haven't looked at my swing on video for years. I don't score as well as I did but that is of no consequence compared to the joy of feeling the ball come off the clubface sweetly and being able to walk on golf courses in the fresh air and without pain. When my back finally gave in I spent several months unable to stand up straight before agreeing to the inevitable operation.

Essentially, my priorities and motivation are no longer on my own game but in helping others to enjoy theirs and to help promote new and more effective ways of learning to play the game. Whereas I spend my spare time reading and writing about golf and coaching, the serious player must just keep his focus totally and exclusively on his own game.

As I have said before, my life's ambition is to rid the game of the old-fashioned and debilitating traditional basics and replace them with concepts that help the average player to move both himself and the club in ways that make it consummately easier to hit good shots. The enjoyment of striking lovely shots and seeing the ball sail away on its majestic flight through the air can be achieved by everyone whereas the classic way of swinging a golf club leaves this as an experience reserved for the minority or just occasionally by the majority. This is the real cause of stagnation in the progress of the average handicap.

My experience with Michel combined with many years of reading, my diploma course in 2005 and much time spent helping and learning from my students, convinces me that we can all play to a better standard as long as we plug into simple, natural, but powerful assets that we all already possess.

I recently searched the European Tour website looking for information about a player for one of my clients who had had his new television installed by someone who told him that he was a part-time player on the senior circuit. I found him and someone else I knew who shared the same family name. I was surprised to see his tournament results from many years ago so did a search on myself never expecting to find anything. To my amazement there were 3 results from tournaments I played in 1972 and 1973. The earliest was from the French Open in July 1972 by which time I had only played a few tournaments in my life.

In those days there was no pre-qualifying for Opens on the continent as there was in other UK tournaments. There was no card that players had to obtain to win the right to play the circuit. You simply sent in your entry form and off you went. My memories of that period of my golfing life are full of failures and embarrassing scores. I took on board so many of the bad things that happened to me that I was shocked to find that I had shot 73 in the first round beating many players who have since gone on to be household names. It was as if I was looking at someone else's score. I have no memory of that day or that round of golf. All I could see during those times was the number of players better than me. Of course, I shot 81 in the second round and missed the cut whereas my travelling friend, Stuart, was in fifth place after two rounds. I was just 21 years old at the time and had only played a handful of tournaments. Furthermore, I had had no tournament experience as an amateur. If only I had been looking at the positives and retaining the good shots that I must have hit in scoring 73. Unfortunately, I became the glass half empty person and denied all my successes and good shots. Oh, how different it could have been if I had been able to see what I was in the process of achieving instead of getting so emotionally drained by the experience that I eventually gave up a wonderful sponsorship with over a year to go.

If I had been coaching this young man what would I have been saying to him after that tournament?

1. Five years ago you were a 10 handicap amateur
2. Less than a year ago you were just an assistant pro working at a club doing club repairs, changing members studs and giving a few lessons
3. You've just shot a 73 in the first round of a national Open Championship
4. You've outscored Eamon D'Arcy, Dale Hayes, Maurice Bembridge, David Llewellyn, the 1971 Rookie of the Year, and many others
5. If you can do this once, you can learn to do it again
6. Tell me about the good shots you hit

Of course, I did none of those things but listened to the negative internal recriminations of my Self 1 telling me that this was indeed proof that I was useless and that playing successful tournament golf was, after all, just a dream. "What makes you think you could be so good, anyway," it was saying to me.

Don't miss out on the positive benefits of underlining the good things you do on the golf course. It was you who hit a good drive off the first tee, it was you who holed that 30-foot putt on the 12th green, and it was you who hit a chip to 2 feet at the 18th. This is reality. Claim them and record them in your 3 Best Shot Notebook or you might end up like me and deny your good shots as being lucky and identifying too much with your bad ones.

Michel showed me that I possessed natural ability and encouraged me to see it and believe in it. He didn't try and kid me into thinking unrealistically but gave me the tools to see things as they are in a non-judgemental and unemotional way. You, too, can do the same in your golf.

> "Modern man is too tense, too concerned for results, too anxious, and there is a better and easier way. When once a decision is reached and execution is the order of the day, dismiss absolutely all responsibility and care about the outcome. Unclamp, in a word, your intellectual and practical machinery and let it run free. The service it will do you will be twice as good."
>
> —William James, Dean of American psychologists, from 'The Gospel of Relaxation' (1899)

Summary

"In the same way that you must choose challenging but reachable objectives, whether in golf, sport or business, good coaches must only promise honest and realistic goals. However, they must realise that the golfer in front of them has more potential to play this game than he or she is displaying at this moment in time. They must be confident that they can do better straight away!"

In the introduction I said the following:

"I founded 'Positive Impact Golf' to help release the average golfer from the inhibitions of limiting beliefs from which he or she is unwittingly suffering. Since discovering the power of the belief system, I am yet to find a golfer at any level of the game who is completely free of negative and self-limiting beliefs that affect how they swing the club and how they play the game. When you follow and buy into the philosophy of this book and apply the 6 simple but powerful basics of 'La Danse du Golf' you will

have the tools to benefit fully from your latent ability. You will be able to reduce your handicap by at least 20%, play with 50% less tension or more, increase your 'feel' for the game and, possibly most important of all, you will enjoy your golf more than ever before."

I fully understand and sympathise with anyone who has found my words not only different but even threatening. I remember being asked by a pro one day about the problems his beginners were having with topped shots. I told him that this was normal for most novices in the early stages of learning but he went on to say that they continued to top the ball for months and that he felt incapable of finding a solution. I asked him what he thought about head movement. "It's vital that they don't move their heads," he replied. When I suggested that this was part of the cause of their problems, he treated me as a fool, turned his back on me and walked off in a huff!

I hope you won't do that, should we ever meet. I know that my thoughts on this and other traditional beliefs are far from the accepted way of swinging a golf club or playing the game. I can only tell you that forty years of looking at the subject from different viewpoints allows me to know the limitations of traditional thinking. Please ask yourself these questions:

How has traditional golf swing technique served me so far?

Have my previously held beliefs helped me develop the basics of a natural and rhythmical golf swing?

Have my beliefs enhanced my potential or have they interfered with it?

If the answers are all in favour of traditional technique then, as Harvey Pennick said, that's fine by me. However, if you only hit good shots occasionally and can't consistently repeat them, maybe it's time to review the effectiveness and validity of your beliefs.

If you think your golf demands too much effort for the amount of reward you derive from it then the messages of 'Positive Impact Golf' and 'La Danse du Golf' have the power to reverse that phenomenon. If you find your shots are failing to give you satisfaction and you are getting frustrated and not enjoying your golf anymore this is the ideal time to try a new approach to your game. What have you got to lose? I can assure you that I have seen many, many examples of golfers achieving spectacular and amazing results with minimal but well-chosen input from their 'Positive Impact Golf' coach.

I once spent a morning listening to Adrian Moorhouse, the Olympic gold medallist swimmer, talking about coaching and how to improve performance in any domain. I was most impressed by his lovely words; *"Good coaches shine the diamonds in people."*

Good coaches recognise the latent talent that their students possess and, most importantly, are expert at 'coaxing' it out of them and instilling confidence to help them realise their potential. I and the other 'Positive Impact Golf' coaches know for a fact that our clients posses both the problems <u>and </u>the solutions to those problems. That is why we need to ask questions in the first instance, not make statements. It is also a fact that most improvement comes from taking away the barriers that traditional golf has put in people's way.

Traditional teaching sees the 'form' of how the golfer performs but rarely sees behind this purely physical facade. The mechanical analysis is often correct but the advice is flawed because it doesn't take time to understand the root cause of the problem. An integral part of Timothy Gallwey's Inner Game philosophy, to which I owe so much, is summed up by his words *"Profound understanding requires attending to what lies beneath the visible surface."*

Often, the poor golfer is trapped in a sort of cul-de-sac of false belief. If he or she believes that they should keep their head still to perform the task of hitting a golf ball correctly then, of course, when the ball is mishit or topped, they are going to assume that their head has moved. Conversely, when they hit good shots they are going to put it down to having achieved a still head throughout the swing or, at least until the ball was struck. The plain truth is that it never seems to work in a sustained, long term, manner and these golfers end up blaming their lack of talent for their inability to play consistent golf. The same can be said about keeping the leading arm straight or the feet static in the back swing, or the club on a straight line back and through. 'Positive Impact Golf' coaches have drawn up a list of generally held misconceptions and have yet to meet a golfer who has none.

I mentioned Bryan before. He knew that he couldn't get through the ball as well as when he was a young man but was still frustrated by his excessively short follow through. He consulted an experienced and well-known pro who told him that he didn't get through the ball well enough. He encouraged Bryan to get though the ball better and more fully. It didn't happen so he asked him to swing harder and faster as if the impetus alone would get him there. It didn't. The truth was that Bryan had lost confidence in his own ability and had become more and more static. He was swinging his arms as frantically as a windmill in a gale but the movement in his feet and body were restricted by the beliefs he had learnt over the years. It was not his body that was in control, i.e. the facade, but his mind's desire to conform more and more to his beliefs together with a lack of confidence in his ability to move and still hit good shots that were holding him back. It certainly wasn't his age.

'La Danse du Golf' helped him to feel how his ability to move and to turn freely had been compromised and, as he celebrated his seventieth birthday and passed from his sixties into his seventies, he began to get through the ball superbly. This took no more than a couple of sessions and is yet another example of how an old dog can use his ability and life experience to rapidly learn new tricks. Sorry, Bryan, no malice intended. I know you are now looking and acting much younger as your enthusiasm and enjoyment of the game come flooding back.

The Gillon Graph

I met Anne, a lady in her late forties, at the range one evening. As I walked past her I couldn't help seeing her frustration and I could see the tension in her swing. She also had the straightest left arm I had ever seen in a back swing. When I asked if I could make a comment about the way she was swinging she was delighted. She subsequently came to see me for some help and this has continued for about 2 years now. Little by little she has let go of the old ideas of straight arms, still head and static feet. Her handicap has come down from 23 to 14 and she is well on her way to playing single figure golf. *The more she plays with a bent left arm and allows her arms to fold quickly after impact, the better and further she strikes the ball!* Take a look at her back swing in photo 19.

This is a pitch shot which had been her weakest shot until recently. Note her relaxed left arm. Photo 20 shows the relaxed, balanced and poised way she ends her movement.

When I took these photos I also wanted to show how tight she had been at the outset but I hadn't taken photos at that time. So, she agreed to mimic her old style. Photos 21 & 22 show this but, interestingly,

Photo 19   Photo 20

Photo 21   Photo 22

not only did she find it hard to recreate, but fully understood just how much strain she had put herself under in the past. After a couple of minutes I had to ask her to stop because she was starting to grimace and was in risk of putting her back out.

Now, I can't talk about Anne without referring to the Gillon graph which bears her name. You can see how her swing has improved and she now hits the ball so much sweeter and more powerfully than before. Without the improvement to her swing I know that she could not have made such progress. However, there was another aspect of her game which would have held her back had we not dealt with it. She was getting particularly frustrated when she hit bad shots or simply had a bad day on the course. One day, after a particularly poor round, she came to see me and was near to tears. She was so emotional that she was talking herself into a state and denying all the progress she was in the process of making.

I suddenly had the idea of showing her a graph of the reality of improving at golf. So, I drew a graph with the ups and downs and then drew a straight line to demonstrate the average tendency. This went up continuously even when the curved line dipped way down. I then asked her to tell me how she felt at four different points on the curve;

a)   when she was on the upward curve,

b)   when she was at the top of a curve,

c)   when she tipped over the top of a curve and was on the way down,

d)   when she was at the bottom, i.e. the low point.

This, in itself, was very revealing for us both as she came up with such words as motivated, confident, excited, 'isn't this game easy,' disappointed, frustrated, angry, 'I'll never play well again,' and 'now, I've had enough and I'm in fighting mode' at the different points. As I drew the same four points along the entire graph she suddenly said, "Are you saying that I'm going to go through the same emotional process every time my game goes up and down?"

"Well," I said, "that depends a lot on you!"

The truth is that the vast majority of golfers go through the same emotional roller-coaster in playing the game. How can you possibly en-

joy hitting the ball badly? One minute you're striking the ball with authority and getting that lovely feeling of a well-struck shot, the next a
feeling of despair as the ball seems to clunk off the club head and shoots
way offline into the long rough. Not only is this an unpleasant experience but it's rather embarrassing, too. It also leaves you with a feeling of
being inconsistent and probably having several drastic swing faults.

Anne's progress is down to a marked improvement in both areas
of her game. She is undoubtedly hitting the ball better as she swings
the club in a more relaxed, simple, natural and effective manner. But,
her new-found ability to put bad shots behind her is equally important.
She can now laugh when it goes wrong. It is this combination of removing, on the one hand, the physical difficulty of her old swing whilst, on
the other, adopting a new attitude to her bad shots which allows her to
play nearer and nearer to her potential. It also demonstrates the unique
power of the Positive Impact Golf philosophy to make such a difference
to golfers.

There is a graph for you to fill out regarding the cyclic emotions in
your own game at the end of the book.

Let me talk to you for a moment about my feelings about teaching,
education in general, and how I see the traditional relationship between
teacher and pupil.

In the past, the teacher enjoyed his or her status as being the one with
the knowledge and the know-how. The pupil respected this situation and,
as the teacher was also likely to be the one who performed the task better, put himself confidently in the teacher's hands. He expected to be told
what he is doing wrong and how to put it right. The teacher also expected
to tell the pupil what to do and required him to listen attentively and do
what he's told. The teacher was at the centre of the process.

This, then, is the old 'instruction' based procedure and both parties understood and played out their respective roles. The rules of this game were in a way both traditional and unspoken. Teacher 'tells' and pupil 'does.' Teacher 'instructs' and pupil is asked to 'try hard' to put the advice into action. But, remember Fritz Perls' advice, *'awareness cures, trying fails.'* Timothy Gallwey spent time in his first Inner Game book talking about trying hard as being *'a questionable virtue.'*

True and proper 'coaching' reverses the roles and puts the student at the centre of the process. The coach is the one with the responsibility of paying close attention to what the student is saying and, more importantly, what he really means. The clever coach learns to understand not only the words used by the student but also how to read his body language.

He is perceptive to what is going on behind the visible surface. His tools are questions and he seeks to bring heightened awareness to the student. Sustainable and remarkable progress stems from this process where natural abilities to improve are activated without the necessity of conscious thought. Take note, I didn't 'tell' Anne to change her attitude to bad golf. I simply found a way of allowing her to see the real effects of her emotions and to thus decide herself to change the way she operated.

Direct instruction does have its place but, as Sir John Whitmore said, *"If you do have to tell someone what to do, you'd better be right!"*

Here are a few more questions for you:

- When you lose confidence are you likely to move more fully and freely or move less in your swing?
- Do you move more or move less when you have a medal card in your hand?

- Are you likely to move more or move less when playing a difficult shot in a tense situation with a club you don't like or do you have the confidence to move more freely with your favourite club in your hands and the ball lying on a nice grassy piece of turf?
- Are you going to swing better when you 'try hard' to control your shot and control the ball with all the tension and stiffness that this provokes?

I trust that you now understand the answers to these questions.

Sir Walter Simpson knew what goes on in the golfer's psyche when he wrote his book, 'The Art of Golf' in 1887. He stated that the way to play your best golf is to be careless! I prefer the word 'carefree' as it incorporates a sense of freedom that I trust you have discovered in these pages.

Many golfers are held back by the fear that freeing up their swings will unleash the devil of wild and uncontrolled movement. They are frightened to let go for fear of being embarrassed by more disastrous shots. One of the phrases I learnt in France is 'la peur n'evite pas le danger' or, in English, 'the fear doesn't avoid the danger.'

In his exceptional book 'Extraordinary Golf', Fred Shoemaker describes and even shows on photo, how people swing much better when they throw a club. He demonstrates how cramped they get when hitting a ball and how free and fully they turn through when throwing the club. (Please take great care not to do this except under the surveillance of a coach who knows what he is doing and provides a safe environment in which to do it). Fred takes the term 'releasing the club' to its fullest degree and displays the benefits of 'letting go.' This is one of the conundrums of golf. How do I let go but keep hold of the club? How do I release the club head into the ball whilst keeping control of it?

The concept of the golf swing as a throwing movement is at the very core of my beliefs and I concur wholeheartedly with Fred's philosophy. If we can only embrace the concept that the golf swing is in the same family as any throwing movement surely all coaches, teachers and players can agree on the fact that good golfers consistently display the six strong basics of 'La Danse du Golf.'

> **Turning**
> **Weight Shift**
> **Rhythm**
> **Balance**
> **Coordination**
> **Souplesse**

When you back these up with the confidence to let go of the old traditional beliefs and, in turn, trust that the fully released club head will produce better struck, straighter and longer shots then you will be allowing your full potential to flow.

I also said in the introduction that, "swinging a golf club and hitting a ball are not difficult. They do become so, however, when golfers apply themselves in ways that undermine their latent talent and inhibit their ability to use it effectively."

Ask yourself what it's like to play well and play badly? What goes through your head when you play well? What goes on in your mind when you play badly? Do you play well when your head is full of a multitude of mechanical swing thoughts or does it seem so easy that you don't really have to think at all? When you play badly do you find your mind asking 'why' or do you just accept it as part of the game and walk on to the next shot, still enjoying the fresh air, the nature around you and the companionship of your golfing partners?

The truth for me is that it is easy to swing a club and to hit a ball when we are freed from negative and damaging internal chatter and, most essentially, free from the misguided and outdated beliefs of head still, arm straight and feet flat on the ground. It is also easy to perform well when you let go of the target and just trust your swing. The day you play 'out of your skin' doesn't it feel easy? Well, this can be achieved on a regular basis when you let go of the clutter that traditional thinking engenders.

You will remember that I said, "I am now convinced that golf teaching has failed to build on his (Ernest Jones) beliefs but has rather become immersed in an abyss of technical, complex and unnatural principles. Unfortunately, I have seen no progress in how the average player sees the basic fundamentals of the golf swing in the last forty years. At the same time, the quality of the clubs we use, and the balls we play with, has improved out of all recognition."

I sincerely hope that you are now encouraged to trust your own latent ability and thus benefit fully from the fantastic improvements in the equipment we use today.

I hope that you enjoyed reading this book as much as I enjoyed writing it. Please don't hesitate to let me know how you get on and, if you are a golf coach and agree with my philosophy, I would be keen to hear from you. I know that there are many of you who feel the way I do and we must work together so that our synergy as a cohesive group can have a lasting effect on how golf is played and enjoyed by the golfing majority.

Please, if you do not agree, don't just turn your back. Get in touch and let's have a vibrant, interesting and open discussion about the art of coaching golf and its future.

I leave you with these words of wisdom from Buddha with the hope that you will take from this book anything *you* consider to be valid for *your* game or for *your* coaching. Remember, my intention is only to give you more options for playing the game, more chances of playing to your potential and more ways of reducing the interference on your performance.

This book is not a prescription on how to play or teach the game and I do not intend to 'tell' you how to do either. However, I strongly believe that the philosophy within these pages has the capacity to help the vast majority of golfers play in a more satisfying and enjoyable manner and help those of us invested with the responsibility of helping others to do so more effectively.

> "Do not believe in anything just because you have heard it. Do not believe in anything simply because it is spoken and rumoured by everyone. Do not believe in anything simply because it is found written in your religious books. Do not believe in anything merely on the authority of your teachers and elders. Do not believe in traditions because they have been handed down for many generations. But, after observation and analysis, when you find that anything agrees with reason and is conducive to the common good and benefit of one and all then accept it and live up to it.
>
> —Buddha

Do you want to be part of something really BIG?

How would you like to join the global movement of 'La Danse du Golf?

My mission in life is to spread the word of a simpler, more enjoyable golf swing. Will you help me?

Join the 'La Danse du Golf' movement here:
www.positiveimpactgolf.co.uk/join

We look forward to seeing you swing!

Brian Sparks
Founder of La Danse du Golf

Ten Practical Steps to Improving Your Golf

1. Practice the 'La Danse du Golf' as much as you can both at home and in between shots on the practice ground or driving range. You can't do it too much.

2. Compare your thoughts and beliefs at the start of 'Positive Impact Golf' with anything you've learnt in these pages and feel may help you personally, especially in terms of the 'La Danse du Golf' exercise, the 'Six Core Swing Basics' and the '3 Deadly Don'ts.' After a few days, ask your Self 2 what it thinks about the book and its content. Write all this down in your notebook.

3. Start your own '3 Best Shots' notebook.

4. Complete your own 'Gillon Graph' and write down words to describe how you feel at the different points.

5. Listen to the internal conversations between *your* Self 1 and *your* Self 2. Modify any of the 'bad caddy' tendencies and begin to transform them into positive and encouraging dialogue.

6. Start looking and listening to other golfers around you. Can you start to see what's going on behind the visible surface? What can you learn from this?

7. Treat every bad shot as an opportunity NOT TO REACT. If there's nothing good to say about a shot, say nothing!

8. Stop listening to and/or giving all that well-meaning advice. Replace it with positive encouragement.

9. Let yourself go to a more comfortable, balanced and full finish. It will lead you to playing a more relaxed and enjoyable game of golf. It may prevent you from hurting your back and neck.

10. Buy yourself an Original SwingRite and practice with it regularly. It will cost less than a new driver and will help you find your best swing and your best rhythm with every club in the bag.

Finally, please email mybookreactions@positiveimpactgolf.co.uk with your comments. I'd love to hear from you.

Gillon Graph

Quality/Handicap

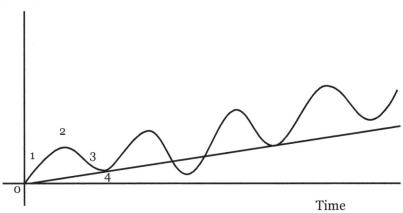

Emotions

1.

2.

3.

4.

Suggested Reading

The Inner Game of Tennis, The Inner Game of Golf, The Inner Game
    of Work all by W. Timothy Gallwey

Extraordinary Golf by Fred Shoemaker

Zen Golf by Dr Joseph Parent

Coaching For Performance by Sir John Whitmore

Quantum Golf by Kjell Enhager

Your 15th Club by Dr Bob Rotella

The Art of the Short Game by Stan Utley

Swing the Club Head by Ernest Jones

The Art of Golf by Sir Walter Simpson

Golf in the Kingdom by Michael Murphy

Golf is My Game by Bobby Jones

Psycho-Cybernetics by Dr. Maxwell Maltz

The Big Five for Life - Leadership's Greatest Secret - The Why Cafe -
    Life Safari all by John P Strelecky

Golf – The Mind Factor by Karl Morris with Darren Clark

Mentality by Karl Morris

Good Golf is Easy by John Norsworthy

The Golf Swing - It's Easier Than You Think by Chris Riddoch

Brian Sparks

Founder & Head Coach at
Positive Impact Golf

Plays and Recommends

Golf Equipment

"I believe that there is a natural marriage between golf coaching and club fitting as clubs must be made specifically for the requirements of each individual player in the same way that every player requires personalised advice for the way he or she plays the game. Furthermore, I believe that all golfers need a little bit of help from the clubs they use.

Ping has always shared this philosophy since I started recommending and selling their equipment in 1975 when they were the only manufacturer producing made to measure, easy to use clubs.

Ping has continually searched for improvements and has, today, the finest range of clubs ever seen in the golf industry. Treat yourself to the best!"

Brian Sparks recommends the Swingrite Original as the very best training aid in golf. All Positive Impact Golf coaches use it on a regular basis as it helps golfers of all standards to FEEL their best and most effective swing.

Our research shows that regular practice with a Swingrite Original not only helps your swing become more rhythmical but also can significantly increase your club head speed.

Furthermore, this simple training aid helps golfers to play the game with less conscious thought and encourages a more natural and fluid swing.

For further information and orders visit:

www.positiveimpactgolf.co.uk/swingrite

Special offer available to readers of this book - use this code when making an order: PIGREADER' at www.positiveimpactgolf.co.uk

Et Legit In Eo Quoque

And Now Read It Again!